God Loves Truth and Justice,
As evidenced in my sister's murder.

J. Crawford

2019

Trilogy Christian Publishers
A Wholly Owned Subsidiary of Trinity Broadcasting Network
2442 Michelle Drive
Tustin, CA 92780

For information, address Trilogy Christian Publishing
Rights Department, 2442 Michelle Drive, Tustin, Ca 92780.
Trilogy Christian Publishing/ TBN and colophon are trademarks of Trinity Broadcasting Network.
For information about special discounts for bulk purchases, please contact Trilogy Christian Publishing.
Manufactured in the United States of America
Trilogy Disclaimer: The views and content expressed in this book are those of the author and may not necessarily reflect the views and doctrine of Trilogy Christian Publishing or the Trinity Broadcasting Network.

10 9 8 7 6 5 4 3 2 1
Library of Congress Cataloging-in-Publication Data is available.
B-ISBN#: 978-1-64088-463-2
E-ISBN#: 978-1-64088-464-9

Dedication

I dedicate this writing to the Sheriff's Department and *all* the law enforcement who meticulously worked this case. Also, to the Prosecuting Team for the long hours and compassion committed to the case.

Acknowledgments

A sincere thanks to the small-town neighbors and friends who had wonderful things to say about my sister.

With much love and gratitude, I thank my son for the many hours he spent away from his job and his obligations to help me search for her body, as well as giving me love and support through the difficult times.

And finally, I thank all my family for their support, but especially my two Christian Aunts. They both bore many sad conversations, yet always brought my heart back to the assurances that we know the Creator of the universe, He loves us, He is with us, and He wants us to forgive because He loves the whole world.

And, He never leaves us, but rather:

> And we know that all things work together for the good to them that love God, to them who are called according to his purpose.

(Romans 8:28, KJV)

Thank you, Lord, Amen!

Table of Contents

Foreword

To God be the glory for revealing to me how He took this diabolical, love-for-money murder, and worked it out, as only He could, to the justifiable end of life in prison without the possibility of parole.

My sincere and heartfelt prayer to God is for all who have lost and not yet found a loved one, may God help you all as only He knows how! Receive His LOVE. I pray this in the name of His Son and our Savior, Jesus Christ, AMEN!

Prologue

The names and locations have been changed to protect all involved and explicitly for the purpose of NOT giving the murders the recognition of their heinous and despicable crimes.

Any Bible scriptures quoted in this book are quoted from the King James Version of the Holy Bible.

Chapter One

The Phone Call

It all unfolded for me in this manner. On Tuesday, September 9, 2014, I arrived home from work to the sound of the ringing telephone inside my apartment. I rushed in to lay my books and lunchbox on the table and answered the call. My stepdad was on the other end, and I immediately realized that something serious was on his mind. Without the usual idle chitchat that precedes a telephone conversation, Dad said, "There is no other way to ask this question then to come right out and ask." My response was, "What question?" He asked me if I knew where Joy was. I said I did not know and quickly reminded him that she was coming for dinner tonight, and asked him why he was asking about her? He went into detail about how her husband Geoff had called him earlier and demanded to know where Joy was, and Geoff kept stating that he knew she was either at Mom's house or mine and that he wanted to know where she was. Dad told Geoff that he assumed Joy was at work and mentioned that she was coming for dinner that evening. Geoff said he was not aware of that dinner date. Geoff then explained that a local deputy wanted to talk to Dad, and he handed the phone to the deputy. The deputy introduced himself to Dad and explained that one of Joy's co-workers had called in a welfare check because she was worried about Joy not coming to work or calling in to explain her absence. Dad reiterated that he did not know where she was, that she was going to have dinner with him and her Mom at their house that evening. So, all three (Geoff, the deputy, and Dad) ended their conversation by agreeing to call each other should they hear from Joy.

My first reaction to the news was that Joy had most likely wrecked the truck driving home tired from her second job. Joy and I had this plan that if she ever had to drive a vehicle while she was tired, regardless to the time of day or night, she was to call me on her Bluetooth, and I would talk to her and keep her alert until she reached her destination. As a professional truck driver, I had full knowledge of how driving tired can affect a driver with devastating effects. She had actually used the plan and called me on several occasions, around midnight, when she was getting off her second job to go home and was nodding or extremely tired. We would talk, and I would try to get her to laugh or think hard to keep her awake until she arrived home, but she had not called me recently.

My first thought to her disappearance was that she wrecked the truck. I feared she was lying in the ditch somewhere. She and I had a conversation about the routes she used to go back and forth to her two jobs. She had just recently told me she preferred driving the back roads from her small town to the larger one where both of her jobs were located. Since I was new to the area and did not know the back roads, I went to my computer and printed a street map that showed the roads from her house to the larger town and quickly got into my vehicle to look for her.

As I was crossing the mountain, I realized I had so many unanswered questions: *When was the last time someone had seen her? This was Tuesday; I reminded myself, so does that mean she was not at work both Monday and Tuesday? Why had Geoff not called before now?* My mind was racing. I went over the emergency equipment that I had in the vehicle, which included flares, a yellow vest, some bottled water, a first aid kit, and a blinking flashlight. I tried to prepare my mind for what I might see, should I find an accident with my sister inside.

Geographically, the first place I came to was the house that Joy rented. I had not planned to do so, but as I approached it, I made a quick decision to stop in and see if Geoff would highlight on my printed map the roads that Joy usually took to go back and forth to work. The driveway was empty, which just made me realize that I might be right about her wrecking the truck and since Geoff did not work, I thought he still might be inside the house.

I parked and knocked on the door. The dogs were inside, all barking at the stranger at the door. After several knocks, I realized Geoff was either not coming to the door or perhaps he was not home. After returning to my vehicle, I decided to ask the clerk at the local convenience store to show me the most popular back roads used to get to the larger town. She looked at the printed map and showed me the common roads local residents used, and I thanked her, paid for my gas, and headed on my way to look for my sister.

I drove the twisting and narrow back roads more cautiously than the local drivers, who were more familiar with the hills, twists, and turns of the mountainous terrain. My eyes glanced back and forth from one side of the road to the other, looking for any skid marks or evidence that a vehicle had run off the road. I paid particular attention to the areas where a car could careen over an embankment and allowed the impatient local drivers to pass my slow-moving vehicle whenever there was an opportunity to pull off the road. I made a mental note to remember the street names I was driving on, and to observe structures that I could use as landmark descriptions should I find the wreck and have to call authorities. However, a dominating thought kept overriding my mind... *When was the last time someone had seen her?* I decided to call Geoff to find out.

Geoff answered the cell phone, and I took a brief second to confirm it was him since I had never spoken to him on the phone, had not seen or talked to him for many months, and I did not immediately recognize his voice. He, on the other hand, quickly became aggravated and demanded I tell him where Joy was right away. I told him I did not have a clue where she was and explained that I was driving the back roads looking for a wreck. When he told me that he had the red truck, I swerved off the road, into the opening of someone's driveway and came to a complete stop. Instantly, I grabbed my note pad, pencil, and started taking notes of the remaining conversation.

I asked him when he saw her last, and he said Saturday. Quickly my mind calculated three days, and my temper started to rise as I wondered why he was just now (three days later) calling around to find her. He continued to explain that they had gone to a yard sale on Saturday to look at a motorcycle, and on the way home, they fought over money. He said the fight was no different from the many other arguments they had recently, and that when they got home, Joy went into the house and he went down to the river to fish. He said he stayed at the river until very late, and when he returned to the house, he decided to sleep on the couch. He explained he had been hot and sweaty all day, and he did not want to take a shower so late at night and did not want to get into the bed sweaty. He said that when he got up the next morning, Joy was gone; her keys and her reading glasses were on the kitchen counter. Geoff said he was not worried because he figured that either I or Mom and Dad came and got her and that she was with her family. He said he wanted to give her some space, explaining his reason for not calling about her earlier.

I asked him if he had checked around the property for her. She was renting an apartment in an old house that sat on approximately one acre of land, with two outbuildings. A river bordered the land, and the rolling landscape made some hideaway spots on the property. I stated to him that since she had been carrying a heavy family load for a long time that it was possible that she could have had a heart attack and was lying somewhere on the property. He said he checked in the laundry room downstairs, the garden, and then he said the strangest thing; he had gotten out of the river looking in the sinkholes for her.

I asked him again about the fight. Geoff said that it was no different from the many other fights they had been having lately and he sounded sorry that they had been having problems. In that same dramatic tone of voice and sad countenance, he said Joy had recently told him that she was leaving him and had found an apartment—but he thought she meant sharing an apartment with me. He continued to tell me that he was going to take a shower, go to her second job, get her work schedule, and then later that evening, he was going to meet up with the deputy to file a missing person's report. Then he explained that he was going to go to her primary job the next day to see what they knew about her disappearance. We ended the conversation with the same agreement as he, Dad, and the deputy had—if either of us saw or heard from Joy, we would call each other. Next, I turned my vehicle around and headed back to my house with a heavy heart. I knew (spiritually knew) that something terrible had happened to Joy, and he had something to do with her disappearance.

Chapter Two

Getting to Know My Sister's Husband

Geoff and Joy came to visit Mom and Dad. During their visit, Dad had acquired pneumonia and had to go to the emergency room because he had overexerted himself and had become overwhelmed from taking care of Mom. In the accumulation of all of these issues, it became obvious to Joy and Geoff that her elderly parents needed help. So, they decided to move up here to help with Mom. During their vacation time, Geoff found the furnished apartment to rent in the old house bordered by a river, they both found jobs, and without returning to Texas, they set up their home. Geoff was going to detail cars at a local car dealership, and Joy took a customer service position at a large food distributor. They were one small mountain away from Mom and Dad's, and Joy intended to help our parents with housework, grocery shopping, and watching Mom, which would give Dad some freedom to leave the house and relax a little.

Within weeks of being in the area, Geoff started complaining that his joints and muscles hurt him and before we knew it, he found a doctor who prescribed several types of painkillers, which Geoff abused to the point of being addicted. On several occasions, he showed Joy where he almost cut through his hand or cut off his thumb and laughed that he did not even feel it. He told her that he only realized that he had cut himself when he saw the blood all over the workbench. His boss also noticed strange and unusual behavior and quickly fired him from his job.

Once again, Joy was pulling the weight of her family. This time, however, the rent was more than her one job could pay for, so she was required to take a second part-time job to make enough for the rent. I had asked her why she and Geoff did not search for a place with lower rent, but she said Geoff would not move. He loved the house by the river. Additionally, she would not believe me when I tried to point out that Geoff was abusing drugs. It did not seem to bother her that he would lie around on the couch for three hours watching TV complaining about how hungry he was, and waiting for her to get off her second job to cook and serve him dinner.

Joy was still devoted to him even though he did not work and did not help her in any way in the marriage. She worked two or three jobs, but the small salaries that she made were not enough because Geoff had access to the bank account, and would remove however much money he wanted, when he wanted, and for whatever reason he wanted. It did not matter to him that there was no money for rent or the truck payment. Geoff would often send Joy to the local charitable organizations or to her family to ask for money to pay their bills.

Through all of this, I could not convince her that he was mentally abusing her, nor could I talk her into leaving him. Over the course of their seven years together, I would ask her if Geoff had ever hit her, and she would insist that he never did. I never saw any evidence of abuse such as being startled by a loud noise, withdrawing, or jerking when someone touched her arm surprisingly. I never saw any bruise marks or black eyes, so I had to believe her when she told me that Geoff did not hit her even though my heart knew he was the type of man who abused women. He had a "bad guy" mentality; all housework was women's work, and it is the woman's place to take care of her man. He was the man of the house regardless of his not working, etc.

She did tell me, however, that in an argument, she had taken him to that thin line. She explained that during a very intense argument, Geoff had her pinned against the wall, and he drew back his fist to hit her. When he threw the punch, he did not hit her, but rather, his fist hit the wall directly beside her head. The same scenario happened another time on the bed, where he was straddling her and threw the punch to hit the pillow instead of her. She said that was scary enough to understand the boundary lines, and she assured me that she would not push him to that point again.

My sister had been married to Geoff for a year or more before I ever met him. She would tell me wonderful things about him; how he was so good at woodworking, and that her dog Dude fell in love with him right away. She said they laughed and enjoyed each other's company, and both felt it was love at first sight. She told me this romantic story about how they accidentally bumped carts while shopping in Wal-Mart, and he asked her about the various pots and pans on display. She was highly impressed that he listened intently to her opinions. It seemed to me that it had only been a month or so when she told me that Geoff surprised her when he arrived at her job, brought her a beautiful bouquet of flowers and in front of everyone, proposed marriage. Nevertheless, to hear the happy stories Joy told about how tee-totally in love they were with each other, I thought... *Who am I to discredit love at first sight?* They lived in Texas, and I lived in West Virginia, so I had to take the word of my sister, and I wished her the best of luck.

Until I met him, he sounded like a wonderful person, and I was glad to welcome them into my home, truly looking forward to getting to know him, but all those positive feelings ended abruptly. Within an hour of listening to Geoff, I had formed an opinion that this man was a liar and a manipulator. I could not believe my sister had fallen for the lies he was trying desperately to convince me of in my living room. He started by first saying he had absolutely no family; no mother, father, sisters, brothers, aunts, uncles, nieces, nephews, grandparents, second cousins—no one. Joy piped up that he was so excited to meet the rest of our family, and sincerely wanted to become part of a family. When I asked him how much prison time he had done, obvious to me by the tattoos up and down his arms, he tried to convince me that they were military tattoos and he had never been in prison. I watched his posture. I noticed he would reach out to touch my shoulder, enthusiastically nodded, or reacted positively and totally into my conversation, and I saw tell-tell signs of manipulation and was so surprised at how gullible my sister seemed with his stories. Typically, she was much smarter than this, I thought.

I knew I was going to break my sister's heart when I disclosed my opinions about her husband. I told her that because he was her husband, I would try hard to be cordial and civil with him when we were together. As gently as I could, I told her that I thought he was a liar, master manipulator, and I begged her to please hear the caution in my voice, and please watch her back around him. They were married seven years before the tragedy occurred.

In Texas, near the beginning of their marriage, Joy had taken out a government loan to start a business with Geoff. They put a down payment on a truck (with his name only on the title) and bought some equipment needed to start a car detailing business, and at first, Geoff put a great deal of effort into the business. While Joy had planned on doing the administrative end of the business relationship, Geoff soon had her working on the vehicles, detailing the interiors right alongside him. He had coaxed her to quit her highly influential job at a prominent college and to work with him on the vehicles. He tried to hire a person or two, but it always ended up being him and Joy doing the work. While it is somewhat common that new businesses struggle, and often fail within the first year of opening, I do not know if their business did not succeed because of its operation or because of the economic timing for that type of business. Before we knew it, Joy told the family that Geoff was not working, and she was once again the breadwinner of the household.

Chapter Three

Major Changes in Joy's Life

In late June, Joy called and asked to stop by. She wanted to tell me a very serious story. She began by telling me that she was very scared for Geoff's life. Not because of all the medical issues that he had, but because Geoff was recently told by the local sheriff that a person from his past was in the area. She started to cry. Also, she seemed genuinely concerned for her own life. She stated that Geoff had asked his handler within the Federal Witness Protection Program to remove him. She said he had asked to drop out of the protection of the Federal agency because he felt as if he was going to die, and he wanted to contact and see his long-lost family before that happened. "WHAT? He had a family?" I asked her. She continued as if she had not heard my question and explained that he had just finished a rigorous medical trial program that was indeed difficult to get through. Several months earlier, Geoff's liver began to fail because he had untreated Hepatitis C, and Joy searched for and followed through to get him into a medical trial program. He had to take pills every day for a length of time, and these pills had side effects such as severe diarrhea, stomach pain, etc. She knew he was suffering, doing what was required of this medical trial, but when he told her that he thought he was going to die, the emotional toll broke her down. It broke her heart to think that Geoff might be sick enough to die, and she sat in my living room and cried long and hard, thinking of that possibility. She kept saying she was too young to be a widow.

She continued to say that Geoff explained how he came to be in the Federal Witness Protection Program. He told her that twenty years earlier, he had witnessed some very serious crimes, and when the police approached him, he told names and gun-running information on many bad influential people. Some of these people were prominent public figures such as lawyers and doctors, and some were upper ranks in some very bad biker gangs. The information he gave the federal agency put many people in federal prisons and some in state prisons for a long time. It also got him into the Witness Protection Program, which relocated him to Texas, and that is where she met him. She did her due diligence and conducted a criminal background check on him when they first met, but nothing showed up. With a new identification in the Witness Protection Program, it would not. Of course, when he told the story to his wife, my sister, he made himself out to be the nice guy, the good citizen, the person just trying to do what was right, which we found out much later was the lie of the century.

As she sat in my living room trying to defend her husband, I was assuring her that there was more to the story then she or I knew. Not wanting to argue, her demeanor changed, and she started to get a little excited. She mentioned Geoff did indeed contact three of his brothers, several of his children, and other family members from states in the Midwest. It did not bother her one little bit that the last seven years had been a lie, but rather, she was proud that her husband had done the right thing years ago, as he made her believe. She understood why he had to tell lies about not having a family, and now he could contact them.

He communicated back and forth with his family over the next couple of weeks, and she was now proudly announcing that two of his brothers and one of his sons were coming to visit them. She was elated that she was a stepmom, had step-grandchildren, and that she was going to host some of Geoff's family for a week. She invited our brother Laith, Mom, and Dad to a cookout while they were visiting so that some of our family could meet Geoff's family. Of course, I did not get an invitation because I had been unable to keep my promise to her about being cordial and civil around Geoff. Each time he and I got together, I would fuss about how he mistreated my sister. I was always protective of my youngest and only sister, and I was not shy to tell Geoff he was treating her wrong. Therefore, whether it was at the insistence of Geoff, or because Joy knew I would most likely start an argument—I did not get an invitation.

However, after the week was over, she told me about the visit, and she was so excited to say that she was a stepmom, and was proud that

Geoff's son, Zaden, had just got out of the military. She was especially excited to find out one of Geoff's daughters had a baby, which made her a step-grandma, and my bubbly, happy sister found new reasons to love life with Geoff. She took many pictures during the visit and said that Geoff, Zaden, and his other two brothers all laughed, joked, and had a wonderful time. She reminisced of the good old days in our own large family, where our five brothers picked on each other, and us, and joked around all the time. She had learned as a child how to handle her own around the joking, and she proudly announced that Geoff's brothers were impressed that she held her ground around them as well. She felt as if they had all bonded and she was happy to have met them, and sad when the day came for them to leave.

To her surprise, a week or two later, Zaden rolled into the driveway in a U-Haul truck, towing a broken-down pick-up and bringing with him all of his personal belongings, which included his three grown pit bulls. She made a quick comment about him being back so soon, and in no time, realized that Geoff had invited Zaden to come live with them. Geoff had not had a conversation with Joy about this, but Geoff had always done what Geoff wanted to do and rarely included Joy in any decisions. My sister loved her husband and got along well with Zaden during the visit, so she quickly accepted this new change. After a discussion, Zaden selected a room that he could claim as his bedroom, and everyone began moving furniture around. Little did she know what changes were about to take place in her life and her marriage.

Almost immediately, Zaden started disrespecting her. At first, he did little things that undermined her place as Geoff's wife, but then he began instigating arguments and fights. Joy was surprised that Geoff would not stand up for her, and very quickly, she began talking about how scared she was of Zaden. Just the mere difference in body size was intimidating, with him towering over her short 5-foot 4-inch frame. She told me that while he did not hit her, Zaden would stand over her and yelled military style in a threatening manner that scared her to death. She talked to Geoff privately about stopping the disrespect but soon told me as well as friends at work, that she began to feel as if it was the two of them against her. Geoff would sit there and watch the encounters, and even occasionally laugh at them, without correcting or stopping Zaden's threatening encounters.

Over the next couple of weeks, she told me several stories of how Zaden disrespected her. She said that one night, all three of them were watching a movie together, and Zaden spoke up, asking his dad if he was hungry. Geoff said yes, so Zaden got up to cook dinner. In a short time, Zaden walked into the room with two plates of food, handed one to Geoff, sat down with the other plate, and began to eat. He did not offer Joy any food, so she got up to go to the kitchen and dip out her plate of food. When she got to the kitchen, she saw that Zaden had dished all the food from the pan onto their plates and there was no food left for her to eat. She was going to have to cook her dinner or go to bed hungry.

Another incident happened just a few days later. Joy had spent an hour or so cleaning the only bathroom in the house. She had told me that Geoff's daughter was coming to visit, and it was difficult trying to keep the bathroom clean with two dirty grown men and her sharing it. On this particular day, she decided to give the bathroom a good scrubbing. It took some time, but she was proud of it when she finally got it done. Within minutes of her getting out of the bathroom, Zaden took all five dogs into the bathroom and bathed them.

He allowed the dogs to shake all over the clean walls and floor, and then made a very rude remark when she complained about his actions. There were numerous stories similar to these, but it was a fight over a frying pan where Zaden scared her to death, and she left to come to my house to spend the night. It was near my birthday, so I was not sure what was going on when she arrived at my door until she asked me if she could spend the night. She then told me about the way Zaden was so mean to her. She said she had asked Geoff for help, and even told him to choose, her or Zaden, and when he could not, she decided she would have to leave.

She and I knew that she needed to leave before Zaden got mad enough to do her harm. Perhaps it would be an accident. Perhaps Zaden might backhand her, and her head might hit the corner of the cabinet, or she might fall down the stairs, but I thought it was a really smart idea that she leave the volatile environment. We began aggressively working toward this goal.

Joy was receiving accident insurance checks from a go-cart accident that Geoff recently had. Geoff did not know about her getting these checks, so she opened her own checking account and began secretly depositing the checks into it. She called me on her lunch break one day, excited to tell me she found an apartment for a rent amount that she could afford on her own, and it would allow her to have her small Pomeranian dog, Pork Chop. Mom and Dad had agreed to give her furniture, and we were collecting kitchen items and so forth to supply her place. Her last need was a cheap car that ran well enough to get her back and forth to her two jobs. She told me she did not want to be obligated to Geoff for a ride, or anything else. She even told me she was considering a divorce, and she showed me her new driver's license. As far as the Department of Motor Vehicle driver's license picture goes, I told her the picture turned out wonderful. I have seen plenty of them in my profession to compare to hers, and Joy's was good.

Chapter Four

Our Last Conversation

The last time I talked to my sister was Thursday, September 4, prior to the Saturday when she was murdered. A lot had changed in her life and marriage just over a couple of months, and our phone call reflected some of those major changes. The primary reason she called that Thursday during her lunch break was to confirm that I did indeed want to split a case of chicken quarters that her company had on sale. It was a great price, and she and I had been e-mailing back and forth about purchasing a case and splitting the cost and the meat. That Thursday she had to put in the order, which she would pick up Friday after work, and during the phone call, we agreed that Sunday would be a good time for her to bring the chicken by the house.

During the phone call, we also talked about her getting her mail, and I was being the stern, biggest sister offering her advice. (She always introduced me as her biggest sister even though she was my only sister.) I knew that she had to cross a busy street to get to the mailbox on the other side of the road, so I was warning her that the best time to get her mail might be in the mornings when she had a little pep in her step. She quickly read into that conversation the possibility of dying and said rather abruptly that I had just reminded her to change her insurance beneficiaries.

As a Christian, I think this was a conversation directed by God; one of many that assured me, in retrospect, that God loved my sister and wanted justice served. Why, in that very short conversation, did my sister's mind think to change the beneficiaries on her life insurance that Thursday, two days before her murder? Then, she got off the phone and changed it! She continued her conversation by explaining that she had Geoff listed as a beneficiary at 90%, and Laith and me as 5% each.

I knew this was a lie because I remembered her asking for my social security number and other personal information to list me as a beneficiary, but I refused to give her such information because I did not trust her husband. At that moment, I considered the lie too small to quarrel over. I told her if she was going to make the beneficiary change, she should go ahead and give it all to our youngest brother, Laith. After all, I explained, he was living the American dream with a house mortgage, car payments, and working two jobs to pay for it all. I, on the other hand, make my monthly bills, I pay my monthly bills, and I do not owe anyone. I said that I do not need or have the greed for money, so for her to put Laith as beneficiary. Little did we know that he would be claiming it so quickly.

Our phone conversation ended, and she and I had set a date that we would get together the upcoming Sunday to split the case of chicken quarters. I had explained on the phone that the upcoming Saturday I was going to be busy cleaning at Mom's in the morning hours, and I had a paper to write for my college class, which I planned to do most of Saturday afternoon and evening. I could not promise that the paper would be finished by Sunday, but I should surely have enough done that she could stop by for an hour or two. I was excited to see her, but when three or four o'clock on Sunday afternoon rolled around, and I had not heard from her, I thought to send her a quick text. I texted, "Hey sis, did you get that chicken?"

As soon as I hit the send button, my heart responded as if I had received a mild electrical shock, and I immediately started worrying about her. I felt as if something was terribly wrong, but I quickly started making excuses for her, as to why she had not come over or called. I remembered she was excited that this was an unusual weekend because neither of her two jobs had her scheduled for either Saturday or Sunday, which meant she was going to have a full weekend off. It was very rare that she got both weekend days off, so I thought that she might have lost track of time working in her garden, fishing in the river, or perhaps relaxing with a movie. I reasoned with myself that she might have decided to bring the chicken across the mountain Tuesday when she came to have dinner at Mom and Dad's. I did not sleep well Sunday night, but I thought my excuses for her not showing were more likely true than to think something was wrong.

That terrible Tuesday evening, when I got home from the first of many drives looking for her, I was as worried as anyone could be. God spiritually told my heart that something terrible had happened to my sister and that Geoff had something to do with it. So, I started calling my family members to let them know Joy was missing. I told them the story Geoff had relayed on the phone to me, and I told a few of my close family members about my feeling of her being dead and that he had something to do with it. I told the family of the disrespect Zaden had been showing to her, and many of us imagined that perhaps Zaden had Post-Traumatic Stress Disorder (PTSD) from his military stint or just a short fuse. That was worth thinking about even though none of us knew the details of his military time or if he was just prone to violent flare-ups. Nobody knew him well enough to make an educated guess, which scared us even more.

I called the hospitals and gave a description of her, just in case she showed up in the emergency room, not knowing who she was. I called the local jails, thinking that perhaps she walked away from home and was picked up and jailed. Laith had also said during a phone conversation that often one hand does not know what the other is doing regarding the different police departments, so I called them all. I simply asked them if they were holding a person named Joy, and each told me no. It was evening, around seven or eight at night when I got the notion to call the sheriff's department to see if Geoff filed a missing person's report and told the same story as he had to me on the phone.

I wrestled back and forth whether I should call the busy sheriff's office just to find out if Geoff lied, but I finally decided to do so. The phone operator was very polite, but in all her efforts, she returned to the phone to tell me that no missing person's report was on record for Joy. I recapped how we came to the knowledge of her missing and how a deputy had performed a welfare check on her earlier, prompted by a co-worker. After further investigation of my story, she said she would get a deputy to give me a call. A few minutes later, a deputy called me.

He told me that Janie from Joy's job had called in a welfare check because she was concerned. He said that Joy had not been to work on Monday or Tuesday, and she did not call in to report her absence. Like most companies, her job had a three-strike absence policy. If an employee did not call in or show up for work for three consecutive days, it was grounds for immediate termination. Janie knew that Joy needed her job and that she had always called in when she had to miss work to tend to Geoff and his numerous health issues. For her to not call in was a strong warning to Janie that something was wrong. I too confirmed to the deputy that Joy had a full understanding of the Family Medical Leave Act rules, and always called in when she had to take Geoff to doctor appointments or stay home to tend to his health issues. I explained that the "not calling" is why I was so worried. Joy was one who was always talking to someone in the family, and for her to be gone since Saturday without calling anyone, was very scary to me. I told him I was calling just to see if Geoff had given the same story for the missing person's report as he told me on the phone. The deputy confirmed that Geoff was supposed to file the missing person's report that night, but Geoff never showed. He said that since I was a family member, I could file a missing person's report. I gave him all the information he needed to file the report right away. We ended the conversation, and he said he would talk to the investigators and told me that they might be getting in touch with me in the next day or so.

Chapter Five

Life Goes On

It was hard to continue living as if nothing was wrong. I was working a specialty job that was going to be finished the upcoming Friday, and I was glad for that. I felt like I was cheating my job because my mind was far from trying to teach my student. I was secretly thankful that my student was a quick learner, had self-drive, ambition, and doing the practicing that he needed without my direct supervision.

I kept calling Dad to see if there were any new updates, and he mentioned that he heard that several police cars were at Joy's house. He said the house and driveway were taped off, and there were several official cars there. I was so glad to hear that the authorities were beginning an investigation into her disappearance. The distraction from my work made me decide within myself that I would complete the specialty job I was currently working on and when the student acquired his CDL license that Friday, I was turning in a resignation.

While the police were conducting the first search of the house; my niece, Pam, was talking with Geoff about Joy leaving her first husband over twenty years prior. Geoff wanted her to tell the police of this history, so he called an officer over and asked Pam to inform the officer about Joy leaving her first husband. Geoff had used his manipulation techniques on my niece throughout the years, she had become fond of Geoff, and was trying to help him through this ordeal. When the investigators confirmed that story to be true, they started treating the circumstances more as a missing person incident then a criminal act. Pam, trying to help Geoff and talking to him so many times on the phone, would later prove valuable to God's justice.

Geoff had told Pam a very similar story as he had told me; at least about going to the yard sale, having a fight, sleeping on the couch, and Joy not being home the next morning. Of course, over time, Geoff changed his story about that last night. There were different variations of his story—changing the day from Saturday to Sunday when he last saw Joy, from sleeping on the couch to crawling into bed with her, and her telling him she loved him. Nevertheless, up to this point, he had convinced Pam that he did not know anything about Joy's disappearance. He acted as if he was heartbroken at the thought that she had left him, whining about who was going to take care of him and his health problems now. He was also talking to Polly, Joy's friend from Texas, and making her too, believe how much he missed Joy and how sad he was that she would leave him.

Trying to continue with my responsibilities, but anxious to get answers, I called the investigators on my way to work Thursday morning. They had not contacted me within the first two days of us finding out Joy was missing, and my anxiety was rising beyond my tolerance levels. I spoke to the lead investigator for a few minutes, and we arranged a time in the evening to meet at my house to talk. When I met with two investigators, I kept reiterating it was the fact that she had not called to talk to anyone in the family that had me worried. I told them that Dad had called her phone over and over again with no results, and each time I tried to call her, it went straight to voice mail, as if it was turned off. Regardless as to what was going on in her life, even when she left her first husband twenty years ago, she had always talked to Mom, our brother Laith, or me and she would not be somewhere without calling to tell us.

I told the investigators as Joy had relayed the story to me, about the witness protection program and the person who wanted to harm Geoff in the local area. Also, that these stories had Joy scared for both her and Geoff's life. I told them to check out the local shelters because Joy had planned to locate the shelters just in case, she felt so threatened that she would need to leave immediately and unexpectedly. I told them about us helping her prepare to leave Geoff... However, I explained she was not really leaving Geoff per se. She still loved Geoff although she was very disappointed and distraught that he would not stop the disrespect from Zaden. I shared with the investigators the stories of how Zaden disrespected Joy in a threatening manner and that Geoff would do nothing to correct him or protect her. I told them about her other bank account, the apartment she told me she wanted to rent, and how close we were to get her out of the house and to safety.

I could not fathom what happened to her, except for the possibility of an accidental deathblow from her angry stepson. Although I let the investigators know that I personally did not like Geoff, I did tell them I believed Joy when she told me several times that he did not hit her. I recapped that at this time, I had thoughts that Zaden may have been the culprit of her injury or death and that I knew in my heart, Geoff knew something about her disappearance.

After listening to me talk, the investigators did tell me that they had called in several other agencies to help investigate. They mentioned communicating with the Bureau of Alcohol, Tobacco, and Firearms because of the ten loaded guns they had found in the house, and the Federal Bureau of Investigations (FBI) and the United States (U.S.) Marshals because of Geoff's history with them. However, with all these new avenues to explore, they were still telling the family and the local news media that they thought it could be possible that she just simply left her husband. They could not discard the facts that she had left a previous husband, and it was possible that she left Geoff as well, particularly because the police had learned from the family and co-workers that she intended to leave. They said that until they disproved that she was not just a missing person, they had to investigate that avenue as well. I told them that I was disappointed, but I understood why they were looking at the situation as a missing person also. I knew in my heart that God would open their eyes to the truth, and I was going to have to have patience throughout this ordeal because if my sister were alive, she would have called someone in the family by now!

Chapter Six

Help Arrives!

On Friday, September 12, my son Tom came down from three and a half hours away to give me help with whatever I might need. He decided that he was going to check out the isolated property behind Joy's apartment and on the other side of the river. That piece of property was a large peninsula, heavily wooded, and easily accessible to their apartment. It could have been a perfect place to bury a body. It ultimately took Tom three days to cover the entire area. Knowing that Tom was searching the woods around their house was a huge relief to my heart. I needed to know that someone who loved her was out there looking for her.

I still went to work, as my student was to test for his license on Friday. My boss was a former police officer, so it was helpful to talk with him in regards to the different ways that police look at and think about crime and missing persons. The local television station ran a spot saying there was a missing woman in the viewing area, and if anyone saw her, they should call the local sheriff's number. They got a picture of Joy from the Department of Motor Vehicles (DMV) recently taken for her driver's license, and while most DMV pictures are never attractive, I was glad they put her face on the news.

At the end of Friday, after my student received his CDL class B license, I went to my boss with a letter of resignation. The letter stated that in light of my sister's disappearance, it would be necessary that I spend my time looking for her, and therefore, I would need to leave my job. He would not accept the letter as a resignation, but rather informed me that there would be a job available for me to return to when things were resolved. I thanked him, and when I got home, I called my academic advisor at the University of Phoenix. I explained what was going on and that I would have to take time off from school to help search for my sister. They understood and put my classes on hold, with the directive to call them to resume when I was able to do so.

I created a flier and used the picture of Joy that the local news station had obtained from the DMV. Our family never was the kind of family that took pictures, so the DMV photo was the most recent picture I had. In fact, within the prior month, Joy had switched her Texas license to her current state license. She had learned that in order to get a divorce in her state, you had to be a resident. So, this was just another step to begin leaving the house, and the picture from the DMV was less than a month old.

God has amazing timing and knows just how to work things out for good! I typed up a flier describing when she was last seen, attached the picture, and offered several phone numbers that people could call should they see her somewhere. Next, I went to a copy center, had a large number of the fliers printed, and began asking storeowners permission to hang a flier on the doors or windows of their businesses. I wrote down the phone numbers of all the businesses that allowed me to post the flier, so I could call them should we find her, and they could then take down the flier.

I was very surprised by how many local people knew Joy and recognized her from the DMV picture on the flier. Many people took the time to tell me that Joy would always speak to them. Many said she made them laugh, and others said she was so friendly. Of course, I knew that about my sister. I described her as probably being borderline genius book-wise, but dumber than a box of rocks when it came to street smarts. She had never met a stranger, trusted everyone, and could strike a serious conversation with any person she encountered. She spoke to the cashiers as well as the managers. She spoke to the stockers, maintenance workers, and janitors. She made everyone she encountered feel that they and the job they did was the most important one. Moreover, when there was a need, she would give a stranger the jacket right off of her back. That is just the kind of person she was. She and I were complete opposites, and while I too am generous, I am more reserved, cautious, and aware of strangers. I am not sure if our differences are due to the age difference (I am seven years older than she was) or our upbringing (she was the first of the second set of children). However, it was very rare to see her without a smile on her face, have a joke to tell, or a laugh to offer. She loved to make people laugh and was very good at it. I wondered many times (knowing how her life was in her marriage and how hard she worked without relief) how she could be so cheerful and friendly all the time.

I remember once, watching out of my apartment's second-floor window for her arrival. On this rare occasion, when she did not know I was looking, I saw her face as she pulled into the parking lot, serious as if she was in deep thought and showing sincere sadness and it broke my heart to see her that way. But by the time she reached my door, she was her cheerful and jovial self as if she did not have a care in the world. Many times, I would tell her to get serious about life and obligations, and many times, she would say to me to lighten up and stop taking life so seriously—the opposite of each other. God, I miss her so much!

I must admit that while I was placing fliers in the store windows of her neighborhood, I made sure to put one up in the shop windows where I knew Geoff and Zaden would shop—grocery stores, dollar stores, and car part stores. There was underlying vindictiveness to add the fliers to those particular stores. The two were always tinkering with the broken-down vehicles in the yard, so I made it a point to have a flier of her at all the car part stores. I wanted them to see that someone loved her and was looking for her. I wanted them to see her face. It burned me up to pass the apartment where Joy rented (which was on a major road leading in and out of her small town), and I was furious to see either Geoff or Zaden in the yard, living their life as if nothing had happened. Geoff did not seem to care that his wife and my sister was missing. Seeing them unaffected by her absence sparked a lot of revenge. I wanted to pour sand in the gas tanks of their vehicles, or break their windshields, pop the tires, and beat the vehicles with a baseball bat. I even wanted to do physical harm to them, but knowing that these thoughts were not Christian-like, I fought, cried, and prayed to resist the revengeful thoughts and urges.

I have two Christian Aunts that helped me when I needed someone to talk too. They lived far away from me and were not completely involved with the story, so it did my heart good to tell them some of the feelings and situations I was encountering. One Aunt has a larger family, with children, grandchildren, and even great-grandchildren, and I stayed somewhat strong and reserved when talking to her. I knew she had many others to worry and be concerned about, but I listened to her Christian heart, her loving reminders that God was with me. She comforted me each time when at the end of our conversation, she would assure me that she was praying for us. My second aunt is the one that kept me on the right Christian track. She would listen to me rant and rave when I got upset, and then remind me in the sweetest and most loving manner that a time will come when I will need to forgive them. She reminded me that Jesus died for them too, and God loves them and wants them to ask for forgiveness. I thank God for them both every day, but during the period while I was looking for my sister, I had to pray to accept the truths they were offering. I knew in my heart they were right, but it did not come easy to my mind.

It took me several days to cover the stores with fliers. Tom rented a canoe to search the riverbanks, and he and I kept in touch with each other via walkie-talkies. The small town did not have a reliable cell signal, so I traveled on land in the same direction that Tom was traveling on the river. We would communicate where he wanted to meet to come out of the water, and we returned the canoe. One day, when we returned to the house, he and I worked a checklist for missing adult persons, and we were able to get Joy listed on a national database, titled the National Missing and Unidentified Persons Systems (NamUs). The national website posted her picture, and the coordinator talked with me about letting her know when we found her so that Joy's information could be removed and filed properly, once we found her. The organization is very useful to families with missing family members, as they coordinate information with the local police, share DNA information, identification of bones and other material collected from the missing person, and they work closely with the police and families throughout the entire United States.

Tom systematically used Google Maps creating a circle around their apartment and expanding outward to cover search areas. At the end of each day, he would go over the maps and highlight the areas we had searched that day, and we both would be so discouraged to see such a huge area left to search. The investigators told us that statistically when someone murders a person, they know and then buries the dead, the body is located within eight miles of the residence. We had not reached an eight-mile radius yet, but we were covering a lot of land.

Unfortunately, Tom had to return to his home and his obligations there. He used his vacation time from his job and scheduled a Friday and Monday off so that he could stay for four days. There is no way I can express how much his help was has been a relief to me. During the times when he was not around, I spent time with Mom and Dad. Both of my parents are elderly and unable to put up fliers or search the woods, but I knew that they too, had to stay busy and feel like they were contributing to the search. I printed more fliers, retrieved a list of shelters throughout the state, and asked Mom and Dad to stuff envelopes. They also stuffed envelopes for hospitals, and to churches asking for prayer. They still had hope that perhaps we could find Joy somewhere. Mom was most concerned for her daughter even though she could not fully comprehend what was going on. Her Alzheimer questions were heartbreaking. She would often lovingly ask me, "Do you think Joy is hungry... Do I think she is cold or lonely, and why doesn't she call her Mother?" It was impossible for her to comprehend, but she missed her daughter's voice and laughter, as we all did.

Over the next couple of days, it seemed that the local television news was not mentioning Joy's name, and the investigators were not keeping in touch enough for dad or me. I am sure that it was simply our impatience and stress that made things appear slow and uneventful, but Dad wrote a letter to send to the local newspapers. We felt that we needed to keep her name in the public eye even though in my heart, I knew we were searching for a body and not someone walking the streets. I had e-mailed the television station asking them to continue mentioning her name, but they insisted that "someone" get in front of the camera to talk about Joy. That was the last thing I wanted to do, but television (including the news) needs that drama to draw an audience.

Tom returned to the search area every chance he could getaway. The very next week, he returned and started searching the woods and railroads tracks, beginning near Joy's apartment and working his way outward. He walked many miles of woods and saw many dead animals. One evening, he told me about finding a dead bear. During a drive on a deserted back road, Tom noticed the tall grass pressed down as if something had been dragged over the weeds and into a thick part of the woods. He parked and followed the path even though the smell of death was overpowering. His imagination taunted him from the beginning, and his heart raced as he wondered if he was going to find his Aunt at the end of the path. The buzzards startled him as they flapped their wings the closer he got to the carcass, and once he got close enough to see that it was a bear, he got out of there as quickly as possible. He cried that evening as he was telling me of the ordeal, and reliving the emotional stress. As the devil often does, he played with Tom's mind, making him wonder if it was a bear, or was it perhaps Joy. He feared Joy was wrapped in a bear rug that her Mom had given her. He kept saying that he did not get close enough to see it fully. I comforted him by telling him we could double-check it another day. As it happened, the investigator wanted Tom to show them where he saw the bear, and when Tom and I returned to the place, it took some time for Tom to find it. In what might have been a two-week period, the entire bear was nothing more than skeletal remains.

I too had a similar emotional response during a search. I got into my vehicle and started a search, not knowing exactly where I was going. I drove the back roads slowly, with my window rolled down, and when I crossed a small stream where I smelled death, I stopped. Walking along the stream, I first noticed one tennis shoe, and what appeared to be torn clothing, caught on tree branches along the edge of the dried streambed. I also noticed what looked like bones lying in the middle of the streambed. There was a tall fence between the actual stream and me, but using my digital camera, I was able to get a closer look at a spine. There were no rib bones, but I counted twelve rib nubs and noticed it was straight, and it had a coccyx bone. I continued walking upstream toward the smell and saw two large trash bags with fly activity and the strong stench of death. In the combination of all these things, I surmised this was a human spine, and perhaps it was the spine of my sister. My emotions went haywire.

I did not have a cell signal, so I took pictures and headed toward the mountaintop so that I could reach the investigators with my cell phone. At a large intersection, I saw the small town's rescue squad building and wondered if the Emergency Medical Teams (EMTs) could differentiate the bones from animal or human by simply looking at the pictures I had taken. I pulled in to ask them. It was a strange request. I started by introducing myself as the sister of Joy, who had been missing from the local area. By this time, Joy's disappearance had made the news, and the story was becoming somewhat of a big deal, so I thought there was no need for too much more explanation. I explained that I had spent my morning looking for her body in the woods and took some pictures of a spine. I then asked them, as politely as I could and trying not to sound too weird if they would look at the pictures to determine if what I found were animal bones or human remains. They concentrated on the pictures, zoomed-in, enlarged them, counted the rib nubs, and either could not or would not say if they were animal or human bones. They did, however, think it was a good idea to call the police. The local police arrived but would not go with me to look at the bones, but rather, explained they would have to contact the sheriff's department for further instruction. They explained that since the sheriff's department was working the missing person case, and the local police force did not have the authority to go with me to the location. It just confirmed what Laith had said about one hand not knowing what the other was doing regarding the different departments!

I waited for what seemed to be hours, for two people from the sheriff's unit to arrive at the Rescue Squad building and follow me to the spine location. As I drove back there, my mind was racing, my heart was pounding, and I did everything I could to keep from exploding into tears. Once we arrived, the two officers looked through the fence at the spine, they took a minute or two to discuss it, and then told me that it was the spine of a deer. They explained that they knew this because of the spacing of the vertebrae. In order to convince me, they went into further detail explaining that we humans walk upright, and over the years, our spine sort of collapses, reducing the space between the vertebrae. Thus, we humans lose height as we get older. I pointed out the tennis shoe, and the torn cloth hung up on the tree branches, and then pointed them upstream toward the bags. They followed me and the younger man climbed over the fence to check out the trash bags, and he indeed confirmed deer remains were inside. The stench was horrible, and combined with the sight of the deer's hipbones, muscles, and maggots; all three of us had to control our gagging. I started apologizing and thanking them for stepping away from their busy schedule to look at the spine with me. They assured me that if it were their sister missing, they would be doing the same as me. I answered a few of their questions, and in no time, they got into their car and left.

I really did not want this spine to be my sister's, to find her laying in a streambed like that, but God knew I wanted and needed her body found! After they left, I sat in my car and cried hysterically for at least half an hour. This event devastated me, and I cannot recall even driving over the mountain to my home. For the next three days, I thought I was having a nervous breakdown. I could not eat, sleep, and could not stop crying. Occasionally, for a short hour or two, I would cry myself to sleep, but as soon as I woke again, the tears began to pour. I missed my sister for sure, but I *needed* her body, and a funeral, and closure that our family was familiar with and not knowing where she was... was driving me crazy.

My thoughts conflicted with each other. Every time I thought I had something figured out, another thought would enter my mind that was as equally compelling and as equally logical. I literally thought I was going crazy! Finally, out of sheer desperation, I made myself get on the computer to learn the differences between individual human bones and animal bones. I learned the arms, legs, and the individual bones of both species because Tom and I had found single bones already, which made me question if the bones were animal or human. I also made an appointment at the local clinic to see a psychiatrist.

Thank goodness, my son returned shortly after this. He was strong, and I needed the moral and emotional support of his visits, although I had felt like a weakling in the last few days. Together, we rode the back roads, usually very somber and quiet, with our windows down, smelling for death. Typically, a person tries to avoid the smell of a dead deer or animal on the side of the road, but we had to hone our smell senses to recognize and respond to that grotesque smell. When the stench caught our attention, we would park the car and investigate what it was we smelled. We had to learn to control our gag reflex as we looked at and smelled animals in all sorts of stages of decomposition. It was an unpleasant necessity if we wanted to find her. We had to learn the timelines and stages of human decomposition. We had to be aware of buzzard activity and investigate what they were eating, and I had to learn the difference between human bones and animal bones. Both of us agreed that we could have gone a lifetime without knowing this sort of information, yet, this circumstance made it necessary to know.

We were physically exhausted from our intensive search without results, and our imaginations took us to unconscionable places that caused psychological pain and anguish. We knew she was out there somewhere, but did not have a clue of the why, where, or how. Was she buried or wrapped in something, and what was the color of the clothes she was wearing last? Did they roll her over a cliff, cut her up into pieces, and scatter her in different places, or did they burn her to ashes? We did not know what to look for; the search was devastating and became even more difficult when the leaves started changing and falling. Nevertheless, we wanted her found, and neither of us would stop until we found her!

Chapter Seven

Important Dates

On September 22, the investigators working Joy's disappearance asked Mom, Dad, and I to come to the sheriff's office because they had some things that they wanted to share. They told us that they had found Joy's purse on the side of the highway. They explained that the discovery of the purse was actually on Wednesday, September 10th. The family was told of Joy being missing on Tuesday, and it was the early morning on Wednesday when the Department of Transportation (D.O.T) personnel found the purse on the side of the highway. They said that because I had filed the missing person's report the night before, when the D.O.T. personnel found her purse, he entered her information into their system, and they were able to contact the correct law officials immediately because of the missing person's report on file. The D.O.T. called the investigators about the purse when the investigators were at Geoff's house.

The police had kept this information a secret until this day, although a store clerk had told me they found her purse when I was distributing the missing person fliers to stores and businesses. I thought when the store clerk said to me about the police finding her purse, perhaps, they found it in the bedroom of the house, and never asked her any questions about what she knew. I knew not to get too involved with other people's opinions or rumors in a small town about such a dramatic event as this story was becoming. However, receiving this new information from the police, about the purse found on the highway, I did take it upon myself to expand the flier location. I distributed fliers as far as a fifty-mile radius in all directions of where the purse was found. I made sure her picture was at the truck stops, rest areas, and at any pull-off areas within that distance. My heart knew she was dead, but if everyone else was searching as if she was still alive, I was going to do the same.

The law enforcement was having a difficult time accessing Joy's bank accounts because she was still being reported as missing, so the banks were reluctant to give personal information about her accounts. They had put out an All-Points Bulletin (APB) across the United States on her, and a representative from NamUs had contacted them from the national database where Tom and I had Joy listed. The police were appreciative of the fliers that I had erected throughout the small towns and said they had received several calls from a small town about twenty miles away, but each time they investigated, nothing panned out. There was a woman that lived in the small town that looked very similar to my sister. I had to take a double look at her once I saw her when I was in that area. The investigators took the questions that we had for them and assured us they were doing all they could, including searching Geoff and Zaden's cell phones.

On September 28, the sheriff told the local news that they had upgraded Joy's missing person status to possible criminal behavior, with unnamed suspects, and without giving us any more details. The state police, local units, and volunteer officials became aggressive in their search for Joy. They had divers searching the river bottom behind Joy's apartment, as well as using K-9 dogs to search properties. The area had several caves that the police searched, and they conducted searches of private land where Geoff had done work for their landlord. Of course, they were limited to public land only, but even that volume of land was a huge area to search, which helped the search that Tom and I had been doing. Tom and I called them to discuss putting together search teams, but because the police needed to search for evidence around the areas of where Joy might be found, they explained that untrained persons might contaminate the location. Nevertheless, at that moment, Tom and I both were extremely happy to see them searching.

On October 6, a man on his tractor, mowing his field, found a cell phone case leaning against a tree stump. Inside the case was Joy's cell phone and one of her work paystubs. He immediately called the police, who in turn let us know the news. They asked that Mom, Dad, and I come to the sheriff's office once again, and this time, the investigators had constructed a large search area map. The map indicated a perfectly circular path from Joy's apartment; south to the location of where her cell phone was found, north to where her purse was discarded, and then east across the mountain and back to the apartment. They considered this path a likely area to find other evidence, and while they had no reason to think her body was within these boundaries, the likelihood was good. I showed them on their map, to the best of my recollection, where Tom and I had searched for Joy. I told them that we had hypothesized the Geoff and Zaden would not choose a place "uphill" or a place where they would have to exert physical strength to discard Joy's body, but rather, would use gravity to assist them in the disposal. I also mentioned that we did not search too deeply into the woods, considering that they would not overexert themselves to get rid of her body. The officers told us that they were going to search the national forests, state parks, and they would ask the public to search their private lands. They suggested that we, the family, also, go on television (TV) and ask people to look on their land for any makeshift grave or unusual digging.

Meanwhile, Tom, his girlfriend, and I were still searching for her. Months prior to her disappearance, Joy and Geoff had an interest in a piece of wooded land and had discussed the property with Dad. Dad pulled up the coordinates of the property, we told the police about it, and one day Tom, Sharon, and I walked the property, looking for anything unusual. We also walked some trails throughout some parks, continued going to riverboat landings, and various places trying to locate Joy's body. It seemed never-ending, but it was not going to end until we found her.

One evening, a girl that worked with Joy called me to ask if I had heard about a vigil being prepared that evening for Joy. I had not, but we learned that some of her co-workers from a department store where Joy worked part-time were holding a vigil for her. We learned of the gathering on short notice, and neither Dad nor Mom could make it, or the family members out of state, but I went to the vigil. There was a gathering of about twenty people, all telling stories about how Joy made them laugh, made them feel special, and many were missing her terribly. Several people prayed for Joy, and the local TV station aired the gathering. During the vigil, I met a young girl that knew Geoff when Joy was working at the department store, and she told us about how after Joy's disappearance, Geoff was trying to get her to come to their apartment. She mentioned that he was saying things like, perhaps she would come and clean up the apartment, so it would be nice for Joy when she returned. Her good "senses" and her mother told her not to go.

Joy's birthday was coming up on October 25, and I met a young man who wanted to do something to try to help find Joy. Kurt was perturbed that Joy was not getting the media attention that she deserved, and he wanted to have a candlelight vigil. It just so happened that a young woman from the local university had gone missing around the same time as Joy. The difference between her and Joy's case was that the local police had evidence just before her disappearance, with a video of her walking in a public place, and the media was asking the public for information about a specific person. Therefore, that young woman's disappearance was receiving more media attention than Joy. However, Joy simply disappeared into thin air, and none of the family members or police officials had any clues of her whereabouts.

I too, was feeling the need for a candlelight vigil and prayer from the community to help find Joy's body. Tom and I were exhausted, and I am a strong believer in the power of prayer. I had written to the local churches asking for prayer, but none of them responded to our letters, so I thought that if I could get people together to pray for her discovery, God could help us in our search. While I was constantly praying, when I was driving, eating, before bedtime, and all other times in-between, I was trusting a vigil would be "...where two or more are gathered in my name..." His name, Jesus' name, which might give us better results (Matthew 18:20, KJV).

We arranged to have the vigil at a local boat landing. I got permission from the proper town officials, and I advertised the vigil in all the newspapers. I hoped for a large crowd to pray for the discovery of her body. I sent a flier that I had prepared to her co-worker Janie, and she posted it to let people from Joy's primary workplace know about the gathering. It was set for Joy's birthday, October 25, on a Saturday. Kurt said that he could get a large bouquet of helium balloons, so I made small tags with Joy's picture and the phone number to call so that we could tie them to the balloons. We discussed letting the balloons go at the vigil with prayers for all the families that are searching for their missing loved ones. It was indeed, the not knowing that was devastating the entire family.

On October 19, Dad and I had made an appointment with the local television station to meet with us on October 22nd at my house, so that we could plead with the local homeowners to search their personal property. I found it necessary to pray hard for the words that I would say during the TV interview. I prayed to the Lord and told Him that I wanted to use the right words to give strength and encouragement to those that knew and cared for Joy. I wanted words of urgency to strangers and homeowners whose properties were within the circle of evidence, to prompt them to walk their property looking for anything out of the ordinary. Since it was the start of hunting season, I needed words that would appeal to the hunters to be alert of makeshift graves or unusual dig sights, bones, or anything unusual. Finally, I personalized my prayer to God, just between Him and me, praying that He would convict those who knew where she was, to tell the police so that we could give her a proper burial. Then, I put it all in His hands and tried to calm my nerves. As we all know, television gets ratings with drama, and unfortunately, this television station picked, chose, and aired the emotional aspects of the interview with only a small portion of time asking the homeowners to inspect their personal properties.

While all of this was going on in the local area, the sheriff's office found out from Joy's neighbor that Geoff and Zaden were leaving for Texas to retrieved stuff Joy and Geoff had in storage there. At this point, and as far as Joy's family knew, the police were not pressuring Geoff or Zaden nor were they acting as if they were suspects. Unbeknown to Joy's family, but as a tactical maneuver, the police allowed Geoff to build a friendship with one special agent. This ruse of a friendship would prove to be valuable during the trial. As far as Geoff and Zaden were concerned, they thought they were free to do what they pleased. However, Tom and I also found out about the trip to Texas, and we were both irate! I called and was yelling at the investigators that these two punks murdered my sister, and although I did not have evidence to prove it, I feared that if police let them go, they would skip town and it may be *NEVER* before we could find them! The investigators assured me that police officials along the entire path to and from Texas were going to be watching them—incognito!

On October 22, 2014, three days after I prayed for the words to use on the TV news for the community, and prayed for God to convict those who knew where Joy was to tell the police, Geoff and Zaden returned from Texas with two trailers in tow. The investigators waited for Zaden to go to work and then arrested Geoff and took him into custody. The only official charge they had on Geoff was the possession of a gun as a felon, but it was a valid charge, and they could hold him on that charge, so they picked him up at the apartment, and drove him to the sheriff's department downtown. They questioned Geoff to find out what had happened to Joy. The investigator told me later, that the two police officials played the good guy – bad guy role against Geoff, with the lead investigator being the bad guy, since Geoff did not like him already. Geoff finally told them that his son shot Joy and that he was there when it happened. He continued saying that when the shock of the murder wore off, he figured he could not help his wife because she was now dead, so he would help his son cover up the murder, doing only what a good father should do.

The investigators used cunning tact and interrogation procedures and kept asking Geoff to tell them where Joy's body was. The investigators kept telling Geoff that Joy's family wanted to bury her and to tell them where she was. After four hours of questioning, Geoff tried to make a deal with the investigators. He said he wanted to sleep in his bed that night, and he wanted a real hamburger. Geoff also wanted back into the Witness Protection Program, but the officers said that was out of the question. They agreed to the other two things, and Geoff told them that they would need a shovel. The police then arrested Zaden for the murder based on Geoff's statement. In no time, the two investigators, Geoff, the medical examiner, and others were driving to the location where Geoff and

Zaden had partially buried my sister. (Praise God!). It was an hour or two before dusk when they all arrived at her makeshift grave at the end of Bells Road, and they wanted to be meticulous at uncovering her remains while looking for further evidence. Since it was almost dark, they took the pictures they needed to triangulate her location in the national forest, taped off a large circular area around the grave, and assigned a police officer to watch the area until daylight the next day. They told us that Geoff sat down at the base of a tree and did not say much of anything.

As things happen in a small town, my son, who was at his home three and a half hours away, texted me and said that there was a rumor on the internet that Geoff was taking the police to her grave. Well, I was surprised and told him that the investigators had not called me about such an important matter, so I told him to sit tight and not do anything because it was possible that it was just a rumor. I told him that as quickly as I knew something, I would call him. I immediately got on the phone with Dad and told him of the possible rumor, not to spread the rumor, but to prepare him for the possible good news, should this pan out to be true. Within fifteen minutes, the sheriff called me and asked if I could meet him over at Mom and Dad's house. He made it sound urgent, although he did not tell me on the phone that they had found her body. I called Tom and told him that at the sheriff's request, I was headed to Mom's, perhaps the rumor was true, and our search for her was over.

The sheriff arrived shortly after I got there and was angry that the information leaked to the public before he could talk to us. He confirmed the rumor was true that Geoff did take the police to her makeshift grave and the police taped off the area so that in the daylight of a new day, they could start to unearth her body for removal. He told us that she was not recognizable, first because of the natural decomposition of a human corpse in the forty-seven days since her death, but he also said that the two had done some things to her corpse in the effort to make her unrecognizable. He did not go into detail of the mutilation they did to her but strongly reminded us that there would come a time when we would need to find out these details.

He answered our questions and discussed the anticipated timelines that the medical examiner may need to get a proper identification. He said that everything of Joy's that the police had removed from their house, such as her Continuous Positive Airway Pressure (CPAP) mask, her toothbrush, hairbrush, pink razor, and other items removed to acquire Joy's DNA, were all cross-contaminated with a male's (most likely Geoff's) DNA also. With that said, he mentioned that it may be necessary to swab the cheeks of Mom and do a mitochondrial DNA match, to prove she was Mom's daughter, thus Joy. He also told us that this method of identification would take the longest time, and offered a sincere apology of the length of time we had dealt with the ordeal already, not that he could have done anything to reach this end any sooner. While this was finality to a major psychological and emotional turmoil, which the family had been going through, it was also just the beginning to yet another aspect of the crime, the legal steps to the final sentencing.

Chapter Eight

Thank God We Have Her

I had advertised and relayed the specific information to our distant family members about the date and time of Joy's vigil for prayer to take place October 25, and I quickly realized that we could turn the vigil for prayer to find her body into a memorial of Joy's life. The local news media let everyone know that with 99.9% surety that the sheriff's department had found her body. So, on Joy's birthday, October 25th, we had a memorial for her at the boat landing. It was a lovely service. My new friend Kurt had arranged a preacher to pray at the beginning of the service, and many people got up to say good things about Joy. Her friend and upstairs neighbor sang an appropriate song, *Don't Worry 'Bout Me*, originally sung by Alan Jackson. Other neighbors said that they could never leave Joy's home without a bag or two of fresh vegetables from her garden, and many spoke lovingly of her generosity and joyfulness. One of her co-workers told how Joy was the first to sit with her at the lunch table on her first day of work, and many mentioned how she always made them laugh. An elderly neighbor told that Joy often brought her food, which the chef at her job cooked. Of course, family members had wonderful things to say about her, and the entire evening was a beautiful gathering in Joy's honor.

The community shared love, compassion, and even people that did not know her until her story hit the news, were touched by the kind words and loving sentiment throughout the memorial. I was asked to speak, but not before receiving a bouquet of flowers, representing peace and love from the community. As the number of people that showed up touched me, I shared my relief of finding her body and tried to give encouraging words to let everyone know that God was with us. I told them I was convinced that with God's grace, justice would be served, and we needed to keep the faith and hold our patience while God vindicated Joy for her premature death. I asked everyone to sign Joy's memorial book, and the crowd dispersed after about two hours. While sitting alone that evening, I cried in shame that I had never given my sister a birthday party while she was alive, and thought about how she would have been thrilled to see the reception of friends at this gathering. If I could offer any advice, I would say to show the ones you love acts of kindness while you have them with you.

Within the next couple of days, Dad and I discussed and decided that we would arrange the funeral right away. We discussed a closed casket funeral and then decided to cremate her since her body had decomposed to bones and very little skin over the forty-seven days since her death. We wanted to finalize matters and begin a closure to what had been traumatizing us for more than fifty days, and we knew there was still the trial aspect to handle in the near future. We called a preacher who said he would preside over her funeral. We chose a Saturday and began to make arrangements. Later that evening, I called my brother Laith, and he wanted to get a proper identification before having the funeral. Dad and I, like the sheriff department, were sure this was Joy's body, but Laith had an uneasy feeling about rushing the funeral, so we decided to wait.

Laith and I worked on her obituary, and I helped Dad with Mom during another long wait. The medical examiner ultimately had to do a cheek swab on Mom and used Joy's bone marrow DNA for the proper identification through a mitochondrial comparison. Then, it was a daunting task documenting the enormous amount of detail of Joy's remains. Interrupted also with the Thanksgiving and Christmas holidays, the span of time was another long wait that tried our patience. It was ultimately forty-three days for the medical examiner to accurately identify, document, and release her body to the funeral home. Once the examiner concluded and finalized the work necessary, we arranged Joy's funeral for Saturday, December 13, 2014.

The preacher was given the new date, and he conducted a wonderful service. He pointed out that her funeral was on the day before many churches throughout the world lit a candle for "JOY" during the candle-lighting ceremony of Advent. In my mind, I considered this predestined by God, and it warmed my heart to think that the next day, Sunday, so many Christians would be praying to God and thanking Him for the joy in their life. It was also amazing that the date of her funeral was numerically 12-13-14, with no planning to arrange it that way, and I too, took that as God's work.

It was a huge relief to give my sister a funeral even though it was not an open casket as with my other siblings and loved ones. The sheriff had told us the two murderers had done things to her corpse that would hinder easy identification, but Tom and I knew from learning about human decomposition, that the time from her death to the time of the discovery alone, was a reason to have the cremation and funeral in the manner we did.

For the first time in approximately three months, my mind was not bogged down with confusion. Up to this point, during this madness, I had often called my Christian-rock Aunt, to complain about seeing Geoff and Zaden in their yard—not worrying even a little about Joy's whereabouts. I would verbalize my desire for revenge, or my sadness about our searches for Joy's body, getting no results. She bore many a crying telephone conversation, and she always reminded me of God's love and mercy, and Jesus' dying for the whole world. Occasionally, she would gently remind me that one day, I would have to get to the point of forgiving Geoff and Zaden.

The evening of the funeral, after all had settled, and everyone went to their respective homes, I was in my bedroom on my knees and alone with God. I cried tears of sorrow and tears of relief, and I gave God thanksgiving for the answering of prayers and the discovery of Joy's body. I thanked Him for getting us through this without a mental breakdown and gave Him my love and adoration for Him being with us through it all. After several prayers, an emotional roller coaster ride, and many tears, I finally forgave Geoff and Zaden for the sins they committed against God and our family. I allowed God's grace to pour over me, confirming that my Aunts were correct about God's presence and love. God does love the world, and He is a merciful and gracious God to forgive me of my many bad thoughts toward Geoff and Zaden. Moreover, I was assured in my heart that justice would favor Joy in this unconscionable murder.

Chapter Nine

One Hurdle Crossed

Having had the funeral and turning that corner, I could now think of the upcoming trial and tried to piece things together as I knew it. The authorities were very quiet about what they knew, and would only on occasion, call Dad or me to the office to discuss things. Dad did make an appointment to find out all that the two had done to her body post-mortem, once the district attorney had fully come to understand the autopsy report himself. The details were grotesque and unbelievable, according to Dad, but I asked him not to tell me because I still did not want to know the details. In my mind, I had already imagined her cut into pieces, and I searched for her for forty plus days looking with my imagination for pieces or parts of her body, a decomposed body, or a burnt or buzzard eaten body.

As sad as it is, it seemed almost logical that the two would have had to cut her into pieces in order to move her corpse. My sister was heavyweight, and my brother, who is an avid hunter, said that dead weight was extremely heavy. I knew that my stomach and mind would most likely be sick from searching for her, and for smelling and seeing what we did, so I refused to hear what things the two had done to her body, postmortem. I knew that I would find out at the trial, and I thought that knowing what they did to her body after she was dead would not answer the questions I had. Using blunt logic, I figured that it would have been almost impossible to move her dead body without cutting her up, because of her size. The prosecutor warned me, though, that I would have to hear what was done to her before it was spoken at the trial, to prepare me for the worst. My mind was set toward the preliminary hearing.

After the funeral, but prior to returning to work, I had to help finalize things with Joy's belongings. I met with her landlord's cleaning person, and while Mom, Dad, and I took a few small memorable things, we let the landlord have the majority of her possessions. The housekeeper had been throwing mail, papers, and so forth into one large box, which she insisted I take with me. I loaded Joy's clothes, shoes, jewelry, and personal items into the truck and donated them to the local shelter. We told the landlord to sell, keep, or otherwise discard anything that we left behind after two or three days of trying to empty the apartment.

I went to the court to ask questions about becoming Joy's official executor because I had a strong desire to let her creditors know she was dead. I wanted to try to clean her slate, so to speak, and now had a large box of bills and things to clear her name because of death. I found out that the responsibilities of an executor would be difficult, so I decided not to pursue it. I knew enough about the law to leave the unopened mail unopened, but I did read the mail that was opened prior to me receiving it. One evening I listed chronologically, what they owed to the various hospitals for Geoff's medical issues, and a few other creditors. It was obvious, but not surprising to me, that they were drowning in medical bills.

One evening, the animal shelter, which picked up and was housing the five dogs since the arrest of Geoff and Zaden, called me rather distraught. They needed to let me know that Joy's older dog Dude was going to die of starvation because he was so depressed, and he would not eat. Her other dog, Pork Chop, they relayed, was also having a very difficult time in the shelter environment. I asked about the three dogs that belonged to Zaden, and the shelter said Zaden's mother was coming from somewhere out west to get those three dogs in the next day or so. After telling them that I was working on getting someone to adopt the two belonging to Joy, they explained that it would be much easier to get them adopted from me then from the shelter. I explained that I needed to talk to a few people and obtain permission from my apartment complex, but I told them I would try to get the two dogs out very soon.

The apartment complex where I lived, did not allow pets, but I took it upon myself to discuss the situation with the resident manager. I explained the depression in Joy's two dogs, and that I needed to bring them home—only until I could get them adopted. I told her that I was very sure I could get them adopted out in just a day or two and that

I had already been discussing the adoption possibilities with several people. One of Joy's co-workers was familiar with raising Pomeranians and was interested in Pork Chop. My son and his girlfriend said they would foster the older dog, Dude, if I would drive him the three and a half hours to their house. The resident manager understood the urgency and permitted me to house them for a short time.

It was all set. I went to the shelter the next day to get the two dogs. I knew Dude from when he was a puppy, and he was very happy to see me when I arrived. Pork Chop had only seen me twice, and both of those times, I had a loud verbal dispute with Geoff in their house, so Pork Chop was somewhat distant and cautious around me. He behaved rather well because Dude knew me, and they both were extremely happy to be climbing into my truck and leaving the pound. I gave the shelter a large donation and brought the two dogs into my upstairs apartment. Dude found a comfortable place on a woven rug near my feet, while Pork Chop claimed the rocking chair where the seat cushion cradled his little body.

Being the note taker, list maker, and organizer that I am, I had started a three-inch, three-ring binder with all the notes that I had been taking throughout this ordeal. I had also saved the newspaper articles and notes of conversations as relayed from family members about what was being discussed on the internet. I had a blown-up picture of Joy and placed it on the front cover of the binder, and the entire book was standing near the recliner where I was sitting. It was probably two or three hours into the time when the dogs arrived that Pork Chop suddenly sat up and looked directly at the book. Within seconds, he had jumped down out of the rocker, quickly came next to the picture of his Joy, and he laid on his belly in front of it, with his paws in front, and his eyes slightly turned but not looking directly at the picture. I grabbed my camera and took a picture of him lying beside his Joy, and it looked to me as if Pork Chop was praying... crying... to see his momma. It broke my heart. I knew he missed her badly. That breed of dog bonds completely to their master, and he was Joy's dog!

I got in touch with Joy's co-worker, and she was happy to adopt Pork Chop. Before she arrived the next day, I went to the store and bought her some dog food and dishes, toys, a leash, and other things that I thought she might need in raising the dog. I told her to keep in touch and let me know how the dog was doing. Unfortunately, the first contact was a serious one. She texted me that night asking me if Pork Chop had recently been around red clay? When I called to talk to her, she explained that when she had bathed Pork Chop, the water turned blood red. I told her to call the investigator to tell him, but he said that if the police had not known Joy was killed in the house, that would have been very important information but now, irrelevant to the case. It did, however, indicate to her and me that Pork Chop was close by when my sister bled out, and it made us sad. Moreover, unfortunately, the dog's behavior began to show other signs of trauma. Pork Chop had very serious separation anxiety and made a huge ruckus every time she left for work. When she returned home, she would find messes, things torn up, and a highly agitated dog. It never seemed to get any better over time, but rather, additional signs began to exhibit.

Pork Chop started having seizures and convulsions until finally, the veterinarian said his heart was too weak, and the seizures were lasting too long—possibly causing brain damage. She and I consoled each other as we arranged to have Pork Chop put down to prevent any more suffering. She had him cremated and put in a small alabaster box, to remember Pork Chop and Joy, she said.

It was the next day when I drove Dude to my son's house. Things turned out much better for Dude. The arrangement was originally set that they would foster Dude until someone wanted to adopt him, but it was within a week or two of having the dog, that Tom and Sharon told me that they were keeping Dude as their own. He is a good dog, and I remember his well-behaved demeanor even as a puppy. He is happy, going camping with them and taking walks or runs beside the bicycles, and seems to have faired the ordeal much better than Pork Chop.

Chapter Ten

The Preliminary Hearing

By the end of 2014, it was time to resume life, as I knew it. I called my boss at the college and told him I was ready to return to work. In fact, I jumped in feet first, and for the first four months of 2015, I worked two jobs, every day of the week. I taught at one college Monday through Friday and taught at another college Saturday and Sunday. I decided to do this primarily because I had dwindled down my meager savings, but in retrospect, I think it could have been a way to bury my thoughts and grief. The only time I had off from work was if one of the two colleges had to close due to inclement weather, and during those scarce days, I stayed busy doing laundry or housework.

It was hard to give Dad and Mom any time, and I gradually started withdrawing from them intentionally. Mom had some paranoid thoughts and fussed a couple of times that she did not want "that girl" (me) to come over because she said, "I moved things around." This is part of the illness, and while things were moved from one location to the other, it was she that was doing the moving. Dad looked into hiring help from an agency, and I was glad that I did not have to go around Mom to watch her decline into the final stages of this terrible disease.

My prayers consisted primarily of asking God that the authorities would get the evidence they needed, and I prayed strongly that both Geoff and Zaden would feel conviction and give a full confession. While they both did readily confess to disposing of the body, they kept insisting that the other did the actual shooting, and neither of them would admit to the post-mortem destruction of her body. I wanted one or both of them to tell the authorities the truth, confess to the crime, and take their punishment without this thing even going to trial. While I had come to terms to forgive them for what they did, I could not be strong enough to love my enemies and try to do good for them, as the Bible says. I felt good that I was praying that they ask God for their forgiveness, and I know that God loves them too. Moreover, I believe that I would feel truly blessed if I were to get to the point I could love them and try to do well to them; however, that day has not arrived.

Of course, everyone was telling me that praying for a confession was indeed a dream, and the investigators that had been dealing with Geoff and Zaden throughout the entire ordeal said they were skilled at lying to police. Furthermore, the authorities were telling me that neither one was showing any remorse. Both had very cocky attitudes and even thought they were going to get away with the murder. They were very sure that they had outsmarted the police, had covered up the evidence well enough, and that they would ultimately walk free. However, God was hearing my prayers that they confess, and while the answers to those prayers were not answered exactly as I had been praying them, they were indeed answered.

The first preliminary appointment was postponed because the official medical report had not been received in the mail before the appointed date. It was rescheduled a couple of weeks later, but that date too was rescheduled because of some evidence that had been presented, which caused Zaden's lawyer to withdraw, due to a conflict of interest. In retrospect, we found out that this conflict of interest was the answer to my prayers regarding the two confessions.

I was praying that they would tell the police the truth, the whole truth and nothing but the truth so that this would not even have to go to trial. While the prayer was not answered as I was praying for it, the two were confessing to their jail cell buddies. First, Zaden told his jail cell friend that they (him and his dad, Geoff) killed Joy and were going to split the $200,000 life insurance policy. The jail cell friend had the same lawyer as Zaden, so when he told his lawyer what Zaden said, the lawyer had to withdraw from being Zaden's attorney. The confessions were being heard by the lawyers, and God had good reason to answer my prayer as He did.

During all these postponements, I kept praying that God's timing is the perfect timing, and I just needed help to strengthen my patience. The police searched Joy's work computer and found the dollar amount of her life insurance policy to be exactly what Zaden was saying to his cellmates, and the police knew they had the two for conspiracy of murder.

Finally, the preliminary hearing occurred on March 26, 2015. The father was blaming the son, the son was blaming the father, and neither was man enough to take the consequences for his actions. They did, however, both admit to concealing and disposing of her body and thanks to God for answering my prayers for a confession, they both told on themselves inside the jail, resulting in a conspiracy to commit murder. Such a charge meant that the police did not need to know who did the actual shooting since they conspired to murder her, and it happened, they both were equally guilty of the murder.

The family had arrived at the courthouse just before the police escorted the two inmates into the courtroom. Mom talked Dad into bringing her, and one of Pam's close friends came to give her support. We all sat on the same bench with Mom the greater distance from Geoff and Zaden, and me at the closest end of the bench nearer to them and their lawyers. When Geoff walked in and looked over at us, he winked and smiled. I thought for a moment that Geoff gestured the wink vindictively at me, but realized the friendship that he had with Pam, and our close proximity and surmised he was winking at her.

I tried to keep my facial expressions as neutral as possible, on the occasion that Geoff and I looked at each other. I was surprised that since this was the first time I had seen them up close since this happened, the first time I was going to hear their side of the story, and I did not have any strong emotions. This was the first time I ever saw Zaden, except from a distance, when I passed the house, and he was in the yard. But while I sat there, I took inventory of my emotions only to realize that I was not feeling anything—no hate, revulsion, anger, disgust, love, compassion, sympathy, or nothing. I still felt the sorrow of my loss, but nothing toward either of them personally, and they were within spitting distance from me. I give this thanksgiving to God because God is good in His forgiving.

The police officials spoke first. The deputy that conducted the welfare check told how there was nobody at home the first time he went to the apartment. He was talking on the phone to Janie, the co-worker and friend of Joy's who called in the welfare check, and told her that he was going to hang up because he wanted to investigate a fire that the neighbors were burning. At the preliminary hearing, the deputy explained that the fire was actually in Geoff's yard and it was still smoldering, and he realized that furniture had been burning in a very large and hot fire. He testified of his second attempt to perform the welfare check when he did talk to Geoff and had Geoff call Dad to find out what he knew about Joy's whereabouts. The Deputy had asked to go inside and look around, but Geoff lied and said the dogs would bite him, so it was best if he stayed outside to talk, manipulating the officer in his cunning way.

The investigator, who was assigned to the case on September 10th, testified about going out to the apartment the next day. Both Geoff and Zaden were present, and he explained that Geoff was calm and collected, sitting relaxed in the lounge chair outside while the officers walked through the apartment taking pictures. He described the entire place as being very dirty, except for a room in the basement, which was closest to the back door. He said that room had no curtains, nothing hanging on the walls, no furniture, or any other items except a mop, bucket, and cleaning rags. He also mentioned an over-powering smell of strong bleach, and the floor was still damp as they walked through the room. The investigator talked with Geoff about where his wife might be, and Geoff told him he suspected that Joy's family picked her up and were hiding her. Geoff even showed the investigator some empty dresser drawers where Joy must have taken some clothes with her. The investigators also talked with Zaden that day.

At the preliminary hearing, the investigator explained how nervous Zaden was about their presence. While Geoff was sitting outside very relaxed, Zaden was following the officers around looking very nervous. When they asked Zaden how he fit into the relationship between Geoff and Joy, he explained that he was Geoff's foster child and the two had just recently reconnected with each other. It took no time at all to find out that Zaden was indeed the biological son of Geoff, and that Geoff Foltz was an alias name. When Zaden was asked what he knew about the last day Joy was seen, he said he knew nothing about it. He said on the day in question, he had come home from work, took a sleeping pill, and slept all afternoon and evening. He told the officers that he was supposed to be working this day, too, but called into work and told them he had hurt his back, and would not be coming in as scheduled.

The investigator also mentioned the condition of Geoff's Ford Ranger. He said that there was a huge difference between the front of the vehicle and the back part of the truck. While the front of the truck was dirty, cluttered, and messy, the bed part of the pickup still had water in it and was pristinely clean. When they asked Geoff about the clean truck bed, he said that Joy often brought home food from work, and he wanted to get rid of any germs, so he washed it out.

What the police discovered from the walk-through of the house merited the officials to return on September 12th with an official search warrant; removing the cleaning supplies, ten guns (most of them loaded), and the officials sifted through the fire looking for any human remains. At this preliminary hearing, the officers explained how the cell phone was found, how the purse had been found, and a few things about the cell phone pings from the towers. They told of several lies Geoff and Zaden were caught in already. Then it was Geoff's turn to give his statement.

Chapter Eleven

Straight from the Horse's Mouth

Geoff started by letting everyone know that he had been nothing but helpful to the police throughout this investigation. Geoff's story was that on the day of the murder when Zaden returned from work, he saw him working on a vehicle in the yard and came over to help. Shortly after Zaden's arrival, Geoff had a neuropathy attack and told Zaden to get Joy. Zaden went into the house to get her, and the two started arguing with each other as to whether or not Geoff should go to the emergency room. Geoff asked for help into the house. Once inside, the argument between Zaden and Joy continued, with her saying that she needed Zaden's support and not his arguments concerning Geoff's health.

I knew that Geoff was lying when he said this because Joy had told me about having that exact conversation with Zaden previously, and used the exact same words that Geoff used during his testimony on the stand. Geoff said that Zaden went upstairs while he and Joy remained downstairs sitting on the couch together. In a few short minutes, Zaden came back downstairs, pulled a gun from his waistband, shot a warning shot, yelled a few profanities, and then pointed the gun at Joy, and shot the gun a total of eight times. The autopsy confirmed that Joy was in a sitting position when the bullets hit her, but they only recovered six bullets and identified six entry wounds. Geoff said that after the initial shock wore off, he decided he could do nothing for his wife, so he would help his son cover up the murder. He told how they burned everything in the room, and together they wrapped Joy in three tarps. He said she was in the back of the truck for several days before they attempted to bury her. He explained that there were two attempts. The first time, while he and Zaden were scoping out a place to dig a hole, they thought they heard hunter's footsteps in the woods, so they left the area. The second and final resting place they dug later.

Zaden took the stand, and his story was different. He stated that when he returned home from work, he saw Geoff outside working on the vehicle. He went over to see if he could help in any way and noticed that Geoff's demeanor was odd. He said Geoff seemed solemn and told Zaden that he had something to show him downstairs. Zaden said Geoff walked him downstairs where he saw Joy already shot up and dead. He said Geoff then turned a gun on him and told him he was going to help clean up the evidence. Zaden said he was afraid of his dad. He had heard so many stories about Geoff while growing up. He was told that Geoff was the sergeant of arms in a bad biker gang, and how Geoff was so connected and such a bad person. He explained that during his short stay, Geoff took every opportunity to tell him other stories of his past, about being in the biker gang, and Zaden thought he still might be connected and felt scared that his dad would hurt or even kill him. He said he helped wrap and duct tape Joy in the tarps and used ratchet straps to pull her out of the basement and into the back of the truck, where she remained for several days. Zaden explained that his dad directed everything. Zaden said he was told to clean the floor downstairs with industrial-strength bleach. He said that Geoff made him dig the burial site, and occasionally, Zaden had to get inside the hole to see if it was deep enough. He said he still sees her eyes and remembers shoveling the dirt on her face.

The prosecutors passed around pictures of Joy's corpse to Geoff, his lawyer, Zaden, and his lawyer, and while Geoff looked at them, Zaden would not look. The prosecutor explained that while using an affidavit to search Joy's computer at her primary job, the police discovered that she had indeed, just two days prior to the day of her death, changed her $200,000 life insurance beneficiary from Geoff being the primary to our brother Laith being the primary beneficiary. Nobody was sure if Geoff and Zaden knew of this change, but my guess is that they did not know. It is my opinion that they thought they were going to get all that money, with the money being the reason for the death of my sister and the deception of their actions.

During one of the court breaks, my niece, Pam, announced that she fully believed Geoff's story and thought Geoff was just trying to be a helpful caring dad. She was making excuses for Geoff that she guessed since he had not been in Zaden's life, Geoff now felt like he had to help his son. She could not understand why Geoff would not tell the truth to stay out of prison! She said she wanted to write to him, and I was angry that she favored Geoff without thought to my dead sister, her Aunt. At this time during the ordeal, I did not know of additional connections she had with Geoff, and only assumed he had manipulated her in the same manner as he had done Joy. After everyone had his or her turn on the stand, and all questions were asked, the judge said that the case would be forwarded to the grand jury.

On the drive home alone from the preliminary hearing, I noticed a cloud in the sky shaped like a cross, and it made me smile to know that God was with us. When I looked at the cloud a second time, it had gotten larger without losing its shape, and I praised God for His power and timing throughout this entire unconscionable ordeal and felt a peace that justice would be done for Joy.

I thought I was seeing some fear in Zaden's eyes, while Geoff had been smug and coy as if he were confident that he was going to get off these charges. While Zaden had been in the military, he was not near the battlegrounds and did not do any actual fighting. To the best of my knowledge, he had not seen any wounded soldiers or any of the gory sides of the war, and he was only 23 years old. However, in Zaden's bedroom, the police found an Anarchist cookbook, a book about poisons, and a medical book about human anatomy. I was beginning to wonder if the fear I thought I saw on Zaden's face might just be his fear of getting caught, fear of the ultimate consequences. On the other hand, the truth about Geoff's past was coming out. He had been a bad biker all his life, and it would not have been too farfetched to think he had seen some serious fights, injuries, and possible deaths in his past. However, if he wanted to be the "good dad," why did he not tell he did the murder too, and take all the blame away from his son?

On April 27, 2015, the grand jury indicted both Geoff and Zaden on four charges: first-degree murder, conspiracy to commit murder, murder with a gun, and transporting and concealing her body. I was deeply saddened when I learned that for the crime of transporting and concealing the body of my sister, they would only get five years in jail. It was the time I spent looking for her body, that was the hardest on my emotions and feelings, and at this point, I still did not know to what extent they desecrated her corpse afterward. The judge would have both of them standing in front of him on May 6th to make sure they fully understand the charges against them, and their right to a speedy trial, giving them a choice to use or to waive their speedy trial option. As I understood things, if Geoff and Zaden did not waive their right to a speedy trial, the prosecution had up to five months to set the trial date. We were looking at a trial date during the months in the fall season, but why expect anything else? This whole ordeal has been a thorn in my side regarding patience, and I continued to pray daily for strength and patience.

The lead investigator and I talked more then I talked to the other police officials. We had several conversations outside the realm of details and theories about the case, and we discussed our religious convictions about how I was praying and his commitment to finding the truth. He thanked me for my prayers and explained that he felt his position as an investigator was his work for God—to search out the truth so that true justice would prevail in every case he worked. We both knew that God loves both truth and justice. I thanked him for seeing his work as God's work, for doing the job he did, and we both agreed that God's hand was with us to bring justice for Joy's murder. I spoke my faith to anyone who wanted to listen regarding my prayers of the two confessions while most of those that knew I was praying as such, some told me I was wasting my time. It took many months later before I realized God did answer those prayers too, just a little differently then I was praying them.

Chapter Twelve

The Trial Begins

Finally, the murder trial was set for October 13–20th, 2015, with additional days available, should it be necessary. The first day was typically set for jury selection. Twelve jurors and two additional alternatives were impaneled. The police officials were the first witnesses to take the stand, explaining what they saw on the first days of going through the house. It was embarrassing to the family to hear how filthy the house was, including details about dog feces and urine on the carpet upstairs. The contrast, however, between how dirty every other room in the house was, compared to a bleached and spotless room downstairs, brought the point home that something went on in that basement room.

The police highlighted the change in the defendant's stories throughout the process and pointed out and proved many lies that they told. They testified about Joy's purse found on the highway, and the corresponding ping on Geoff's cell phone from the tower in the same location, and the final tower location on the mountain, which made a complete circle from their house to the items and back home again. As ironic as it was, this entire disposal happened the day that the deputy conducted the welfare check on Joy. It was not until the deputy stopped by that the two felt the urgency and started to get rid of the evidence.

On the first day, some of Joy's co-workers had to testify on the stand, including Janie who initially called in the welfare check on Joy. She explained that she knew Joy needed her job, and Joy always called in when she was absent from work. She said that Joy had told her the last Friday, that she had something very important to tell Janie. Janie said she knew Joy was getting things together to leave the volatile situation. Joy had told several people at work how disrespectful and violent Zaden had been toward her, and that Geoff was not doing anything to stop the behavior. Another co-worker told of a story about Joy and Geoff looking at some puppies, and how during the visit, Geoff spoke very disrespectfully and degradingly to Joy in front of her. She also mentioned how quickly Geoff showed up at Joy's job to talk to the Human Resources Department about dropping Joy off the medical insurance, so he could afford to buy Cobra to continue insurance coverage on him. Finally, a third woman from Joy's work testified to Joy changing her beneficiary and explaining the amounts she carried, as well as the legalities of collecting the money.

The second day of the trial, Joy's upstairs neighbor testified about seeing Geoff at contradicting times to Geoff's testimony, seeing Geoff wearing black latex gloves, and acting very nervous. When the neighbor tried to hold a casual conversation with Geoff by asking him if he had found Joy, Geoff responded to him... "You know what they say, here today and gone tomorrow." He also testified about smelling a strong odor of bleach and the fighting he could hear that occurred between Geoff and Joy, and Zaden and Joy. Even though Geoff was telling the police that Joy often left for several days at a time, the police pointed out that this time she left her CPAP mask, her medications, reading glasses, and many other personal items. Near the end of the second day, evidence was presented that Geoff had been in the Federal Witness Protection Program and under the marshal's care. His removal from the program began when in March of 2014, Geoff went to a gun store and tried to buy a gun. Since he was using his alias name, he figured he would come back clean on the background check. However, his alias name flagged the Federal Marshals. They, in turn, came to talk to Geoff and took him out of the program. He did not ask for removal by his own free will because he thought he was dying, as he successfully told to my sister, which got her so terribly upset.

It was about the third day of the trial, where Geoff's biker past was uncovered. An ATF official explained Geoff's role of a sergeant of arms in a biker gang, as an enforcer of the gang rules. He explained how Geoff had been caught cooking meth and turned informant with knowledge of gunrunning to beat those charges, and he entered into the Federal Witness Protection Program. His son Zaden would have been two years old when Geoff received his new identity and relocated.

Zaden testified later that he spent most of his life looking for Geoff, and the only information he could find was a short story about Geoff getting caught with drugs that was written in a book about the lifestyle of bikers titled Out in Bad Standing, by Edward Winterholder.

During the investigation of Joy's disappearance, about six days after the death of Joy, Geoff asked the special agent from the U.S. Marshal's office for a secret meeting with him. Geoff thought he had made a connection with this special agent and Geoff wanted to meet with him to ask back into the biker world as an informant. Geoff said he could easily train his son to be an informant and the two could work for them again. The special agent who was secretly taping the conversation kept bringing the conversation back around to where Joy might be or what happened to her. Geoff said he thought bikers had kidnapped her in retaliation for him helping the Feds in the past. The expert said that bikers would not steal Geoff's wife, but if they wanted Geoff, they would take him out. The conversation ended with the special agent telling Geoff he would consider letting Geoff back in but only after there was a resolution about Joy. At this time, her disappearance was still being investigated as either she simply left her husband or possibly a crime had occurred. The special agent was later asked if he did indeed have any plans of putting Geoff back into the biker world as an informant, and the special officer said not at all. He explained that Geoff had been out of the gang life for many years, and things were so much different now than it was back then. He explained that bikers do not have any loyalty now; they jump from one gang to another, and things were just too different for Geoff to be any help.

It was also on this day of the trial that we learned the police removed ten guns from Zaden's unlocked bedroom, and most of them were loaded. Joy did not like guns and was probably upset about Zaden bringing them in, but she never said anything to me about them. The police told of finding an Anarchist cookbook, a hand-written Mujahedeen cookbook (a book about painful and horrifying poisons), a personal journal, and a human anatomy book in Zaden's bedroom as well. In the personal journal were several pages with detailed hand-written information about a poisoned rabbit's death, very similar to what was written in the Mujahedeen cookbook. When asked about them, Zaden explained the books as simple curiosity of what devices the enemies in Iraq were using, and he acquired them while in the military. After serious investigation, the officials did not consider Zaden a national threat against the country, even though he had these materials and guns.

About a month before Joy's disappearance, she and I had a long texting conversation while she was sitting at the doctor's office during one of Geoff's doctor visits. She was highly upset that Zaden was with them, and that he insisted on going into the examining room with them. He was also asking the doctor medical questions. Joy was asking me in her texts what did I think, and I told her it sounded like Geoff was going to let Zaden become his medical executor to take care of him. I warned her to watch her back because it sounded to me like they were working on pushing her out. My imagination was thinking that perhaps they would change the locks on the door or simply ask her to leave. I never thought things would escalate to murder, but I did not know she had a $200,000 life insurance policy either. During this day of the trial, the investigator read those text messages to the jury. It was proof that the two were indeed working on something together without telling Joy what was going on.

When the forensic examiner explained how and in what condition they found Joy's body, our family was extremely disturbed. It was unclear if her skull was left out of the ground intentionally, or if perhaps, the rain had washed away the dirt. All of her body was wrapped in tarps except for her head. It was unclear to the experts if Geoff and/or Zaden caused her skull to crack open, or if it were animal predators that caused the crack. Geoff had explained that he cut the tarp from around her head to give his wife one last kiss, but the prosecutors surmised that he cut the tarp to speed up decomposition. Geoff said he did not kiss her because when they let her roll down the hill, her eyes popped out of their sockets, and Geoff could not kiss her like that. The examiner explained how the police roped off the area and unburied her body the next day. Without removing the tarps, her body was put into the body bag and sent it to the medical examiner.

I testified after the forensic examiner. Questions about the conversation Joy and I had regarding the changing of the life insurance beneficiary, and questions about how often Joy came to visit and stay the night were asked and answered. She had only spent the night the one time when Zaden and Joy fought about the frying pan, and I explained that we were indeed trying to get her away from the violent situation at home. I explained why I had filed the missing person's report, and described the numerous efforts made to find her since the day we found out. The prosecutor wanted to hear about the one and only conversation that I had with Geoff. Each time I was sworn in, I had to raise my right hand and "swear to tell the truth, the whole truth, and nothing but the truth, so help me God," and I always answered, "So help me God—I do." I am fully aware of God's law about not bearing false witness, so each time I was given the opportunity, I asked for His help when I spoke.

Other forensic experts testified on this day. One expert of skull and skeletal remains told where and how the two murderers cut her up. They cut her throat from ear to ear and completely removed the bottom jaw, and pulled her upper teeth. They cut off her forearms just above the elbow. Since we do not know the truth, we can only assume that these things were done to make identification of the body harder. Some of the gross things they did to her, we are guessing were done to pretend retaliation from the other bikers, but no one knows for sure why they took the skin off her face; cut off her breasts and gutted her like an animal. They broke her ribs and removed all of the lower organs, leaving the lungs and heart. It is my opinion that they simply ran out of time, and I think that without a doubt, they would have gotten to the lungs and heart also if they had time. None of her removed body parts were found, and the investigators believe that they threw her organs into the fire, and that was what caused the fire to burn so hot and so high into the treetops—sort of like meat fat hitting the flame on the grill and shooting the flames high and hot. The skeletal expert did find canine bite marks on her left humerus. He explained that the arm was wrapped with the tarp, so animals at the gravesite had not gotten under the tarp. Therefore, it was surmised that the dogs at the house had to be the culprits chewing on her bone.

Finally, the medical examiner described her findings. She supplied pictures to show to the jury, but I refused to look at any. It was not even a temptation considering I knew it had all been done postmortem and was simply Geoff and Zaden's despicable grotesque disrespect. It was my thought that I had already dreamed and imagined my sister's body in various stages of decomposition and decay, so it was not necessary for me to see her in those ways. I am not sure if our brother Laith looked at the pictures or not, but even when I suggested that nobody look, both Tom and Dad looked at them all. Primarily, the doctor explained the bullet entries, how the tarps were wrapped and taped around her body, and what could be learned about the cut marks and the handy work similar to skinning a deer. It was officially determined that Joy died from the gunshot wounds; however, as the medical examiner explained it, none of the bullets were instantly fatal. That meant to me that she did not die quickly. In one sense, this was a relief to me because although I knew Joy knew Jesus, I was not sure how recently she had talked to Him. Geoff had said at one time that he left her lying on the couch for six hours before returning to her, so I am convinced in my heart that she had a sincere talk with our Lord before she closed her eyes for the last time.

A weekend break from the trial arrived at just the right time. Everyone needed a break, even though nobody slept well over the weekend. Still, it was good to walk away and not have to return until Monday. Originally, the prosecutor thought that we could finish the case in just five days, but now it looked like it was going to continue for a few more days.

When Monday arrived, the testimony began again with the lead investigator. He tied together the path that the two took to discard Joy's possessions and connected the telephone ping records of whom Geoff was talking to during the time they were discarding the items. It was a perfectly complete circle from where they left their house, went south to the location where he threw the cell phone into the farmer's field. I consider God's presence here because even though Geoff threw the cell phone out of a moving vehicle, it landed leaning perfectly against a tree stump. Then, the farmer who was mowing his field with his tractor, pulling the cutter behind him, just happened to see this small cell phone case leaning against the tree stump. Inside the case were her cell phone (battery missing) and a paystub from the second job that Joy worked. Since she had been in the news, the farmer knew to call in the discovery right away. Then, the two took the highway north where his friend and Joy's niece, Pam, happened to be talking to Geoff when he was throwing Joy's purse out of the window.

I drove that road every day back and forth to work, and after being told the mile marker where the purse was located, I noticed that it was at one of the few secluded areas located right in a bend of the road where a tall mound of dirt separated the north from the south side of the highway. The D.O.T. person who found it said that the purse was not lying down but sitting up as if it was intentionally placed on the ground and almost against the guardrail. The investigator emptied the contents for the jury to see, and it included a wallet with identification, a bank account book, and a few more small things. The contents of the purse were organized and orderly. On Geoff and Zaden's excursion, they then turned off the same exit I use, and that road heads back east across the small mountain where an officer called to ask Geoff some questions. This ping from a different cell tower changed during the phone call, indicating that they crossed the mountain and turned on the road that would lead them right back to their apartment. This was the circular map the police had shown the family and me when we were called into the sheriff's office.

The police had calculated how much Joy and Geoff were in debt. They estimated approximately $81,000 in medical expenses, which was due to at least 90% of Geoff's health problems. They were being sued by at least one medical facility for non-payment. Joy had a student loan to pay off, and there were back taxes that the Internal Revenue Service was trying to collect. While Joy had attempted filing for bankruptcy earlier in the year, a required class they attended had not been filed properly and was showing incomplete, and her bankruptcy was stalled.

Geoff had told the police several lies about where he had discarded the gun. He said that he disassembled the gun and discarded it, piece by piece, over several different roads, and while the police walked the routes with metal detectors, they did not find any pieces. There was media coverage of the state and local police searching in a swamp directly off a major road, but the gun was not recovered from there either. The medical examiner and another forensic examiner mentioned that the bullets used were hollow-point. The bullets were hollow-point bullets that cause the most damage to its target. When the hollow-point bullet hits its target, the damage spreads wider, and for the most part, the bullet would typically stay inside the target. Our examiner found a total of six bullets and six entry wounds.

Finally, two cellmates that heard Zaden tell his story about splitting the insurance money, testified to what they heard and how Zaden proudly told the story. Both were criminals themselves, and when asked why they would tell their lawyer, one of the men admitted that he was a thief and had some charges against him for drugs. However, he continued, he said he did have morals and what is wrong is wrong, and killing someone for their life insurance money was wrong in his eyes. Both of the men said they got into a lot of trouble with other inmates because other inmates now considered them snitches, but they did not want Joy's murder on their conscience.

The two primary investigators recapped all the variables of both Geoff and Zaden's different interviews. They highlighted to the jury how many times the stories changed and that both Geoff and Zaden were lying all the way through the trial. Geoff allowed more interviews with the investigators than Zaden did, but the stories about even the smallest details changed repeatedly. Before the day's testimonies were over, the investigators discredited just about everything that Geoff and Zaden had said. We all know that telling the truth is much easier than telling a lie. The truth does not change because it is factual and has specific details, whereas a lie constantly changes because it is hard to remember how you told the lie the first time. My family has concluded we will never know the truth. I am sure that even the two murderers have thought through the situations from so many different angles, that they, themselves, probably do not know what the truth is anymore.

Dad had to testify to several things. He is Joy's, Laith's, and my stepdad and had been married to our Mom for approximately eleven years when this murder happened. He testified as to the all the jobs Joy had worked since they moved up from Texas, and to her consistently calling to talk to her Mother even though Mom was having a hard time holding a conversation. He confirmed that she visited and attended to her Mother and said it was uncharacteristic of her to not to keep in touch with family. He explained that Geoff was not as frequent a visitor, and told of the few times Geoff and Zaden visited before this incident. There were three phone conversations with Dad and Geoff, since the disappearance of Joy. The one where the deputy talked with him, and then the following Sunday, he called Geoff and asked what was going on. There was one other attempt on Geoff's part, calling Dad to see if he could come over and Dad said he did not want him around.

Dad told about meeting some of Geoff's family at the cookout, and a time when Geoff and Joy came over to borrow money. Geoff asked Dad for some money when they were downstairs together, while Joy got Mom alone upstairs and borrowed money from her as well. It totaled $6,000, and I remember Joy calling me and telling me that for the first time in a long time, she had paid every one of her bills. I knew not to ask where she got the money, and frankly, I did not want to know. Mom and Dad had paid many of their bills, but I too had paid the truck payment often and several times paid their rent, two and three months at a time. Still, we could not get Joy to see the abuse. Finally, the prosecution rested. The judge told the jury that this would carry over for one or two more days and prepared them for the extended time needed. Motions made from all attorneys wrapped up the court proceedings for the day, and everyone agreed that they would be ready tomorrow. Both Geoff and Zaden were going to testify as well as Zaden's Mom, Tonya.

Chapter Thirteen

Geoff's and Zaden's Testimony

On Tuesday, October 21, 2015, Geoff was the first to take the stand. He began by confirming all that was said about his biker past, agreed it was true, and he was in the Federal Witness program. He agreed that biker women are considered less than the family dog and if someone called their own girlfriend a very derogatory name that it would not offend anyone in the gang. He explained his role as the sergeant of arms and that it was his responsibility to enforce the gang rules. He was quick to tell us that he and Joy had met on the internet, but that she had made up the story about meeting in Wal-Mart. She knew the majority of her family knew the dangers of dating from the internet and would have disapproved. He talked about his detailing business in Texas, their quick courtship, his proposal, and their marriage. His health was discussed, and he said that he had severe diabetes, nerve damage from diabetes, and confirmed his liver was failing due to hepatitis C until Joy got him into the medical trial that cured his liver. He talked about going into the gun shop to buy a rifle and confirmed that he thought his alias name would show a clean slate on the background check. He also admitted that the paperwork was flagged by the Federal Bureau and they removed him from the program.

He was asked about his and Joy's money problems, and he told them about them trying to file bankruptcy, but somehow the class they took online did not file it properly. He said Joy was trying to get it resolved. He talked about his two brothers coming to visit him and seeing Zaden for the first time in twenty years. He then started saying bad things about Zaden. Geoff said Zaden was disrespectful to everyone, including him. He said that his son had an attitude that everything was his and that he ran the place. Geoff confirmed most of the stories that Joy's co-workers and I had told about the disrespect of Zaden, and he was throwing his son under the bus, so to speak.

He said that he and Joy went to the yard sale and had a fight over money. He said that he wanted Joy to ask her parents for the money for the motorcycle they saw at the yard sale, and Joy refused. He kept thinking of ways that Joy could get the money, and never said anything about him getting a job and paying for it himself. He said when they got home, Zaden was already back from his Wal-Mart job, and he showed pictures of the motorcycle to Zaden. He asked his son if he would lend him the $6,000, but Zaden said no because he was still paying off his bike. Then he said Joy went inside, and he and Zaden began working on the truck together. After a few minutes, Geoff said he had a neuropathy attack and told Zaden to get Joy. Joy was asking Geoff questions, just trying to keep him alert and talking. Geoff asked for help into the house and said he was overdosing on the Fentanyl patch. Joy was saying that he needed to go to the emergency room, but Geoff said he did not want to go, and that was when Zaden got into an argument with Joy.

Geoff said the argument got bad and he tried to calm them both down. Then Zaden went upstairs, and he and Joy started calming down and relaxing. When Zaden returned a few minutes later, Joy spoke up and said it would be very nice if he would give her some support with his dad's health, and Zaden pulled out a gun. Geoff said he fired one warning shot, called out some profanities and then unloaded the gun into Joy's torso. Geoff said he reached for the phone to call 9–1–1, but Zaden hit it out of his hand. Then Zaden began begging his dad to tell him what to do. Geoff said he leaned over, kissed his wife, and went outside. Zaden followed, and within a few minutes, he and Zaden got into an argument and Geoff punched Zaden. Zaden then fell on his knees and told his dad to beat him. Geoff said he did not know what to do. Geoff said all the animals were freaking out, so he told Zaden to take Pork Chop and the rest of the dogs upstairs. He decided that he could do nothing for his wife, she was dead, and so he would help his son get rid of the evidence.

Geoff said they rolled Joy in the tarps and duct-taped them. He said that Zaden got Joy's shoulders onto the back of the truck and together they slid her into the truck—whole and not cut up or dismantled. Geoff made it sound like they did that rather quickly, however, elsewhere he had told police that he went outside and stayed out of the basement where she lay, for six hours or so before returning.

He continued, saying that the next day, the two of them carried all the furniture and everything from that room out to the burn pit and started the fire. Geoff then told all these routes that he and Zaden drove to throw away the gun parts, one piece at a time. Geoff said they attempted to bury her body the night of the 8th, but thought they heard hunters, so they aborted and brought her back home. Early the next morning, they took her out again to a different location and buried her at the end of Bells Road. He said it took three or four hours and nobody walked by the whole time they were there.

He said Joy was wrapped like a mummy and neither of them could carry her, so they lowered the tailgate, turned her feet out and just pushed her out of the truck, like dumping the trash, he said. He described the action of her body rolling as boom didity... boom didity... boom! Then he said she bounced a few times before landing sideways against a tree. She was close enough to the makeshift grave that they could together drag her into the hole. He said she was still very much whole, and when asked about the postmortem dismantling, skinning, and gutting her, he said that Zaden must have returned to the makeshift grave and did it. He said Zaden was the one that mentioned getting the bullets out of the body, so Geoff cut open the tarp and started digging around in her body to retrieve the bullets. They both layered rocks and dirt until they covered her with what Geoff thought was two feet of dirt. However, when the police arrived at the makeshift grave, her head was exposed, and all of her white hair had blown lose all over the place. The experts could not determine if her skull was exposed intentionally, or if rain washed the dirt away and exposed her head.

Geoff said he did not take the purse or cell phone to discard them until after the deputy had visited the house. For the most part, Geoff admitted to and told the general truth about everything, even things that made him look bad, like his biker activity, not working, and having money problems, etc. When asked about the actual shooting of Joy, he insisted that Zaden did it by just going crazy and firing. Each attorney had his or her turns questioning Geoff, and after about three or four hours of testimony, it was Zaden's turn to take the stand.

Zaden Takes the Stand

Zaden's lawyer stated right off, asking Zaden if he murdered Joy, even accidentally, and Zaden answered with a strong "No". Zaden agreed that he helped Geoff conceal the body and the evidence of the murder, but insisted that he was held at gunpoint by his father, Geoff. He then explained his relationship with Geoff and explained that he had originally told the police that he was Geoff's foster son because of his father being in the Federal Witness Protection Program, and he was not sure that he could tell the truth about it since his last name was Geoff's original last name. He told the jury about his military stint and that he was released because of an injury to his shoulder, back, and neck that made him no longer physically fit for military duties. He was stationed in Kansas, Kentucky, and Georgia, but he was deployed to two places in Iraq in the year 2010–2011. He did not see any fighting and insisted that he had never even pointed a weapon at another person. He was released from the military in November 2011.

Zaden did say that it was the military, which sparked his interest in guns, and he had begun a collection that included the ten guns he brought to Geoff and Joy's house. He told the jury that he began searching for his dad when he was 15 years old, had learned how to skip-trace and had even lied to the military to get them to try to find him. They finally got together when Geoff started calling around to his brothers, who in turn told Zaden that his dad had contacted them. Zaden insisted on coming to visit with the two other brothers. He was very excited to meet his dad, who had left when he was two years old. His mother begged him not to reconnect with his dad, but she was just wasting her breath as far as he was concerned. He was going to see the hero dad that he had searched for so long.

He told how during that first week's visit, everyone, including Joy, was happy-go-lucky, laughing, and getting along with each other. Zaden said that he met our parents and that while Joy was working, Geoff started talking about him moving in and living there. Zaden was under the impression that Geoff had discussed the situation over with Joy and that she had approved. He did not realize that conversation never took place until he pulled into the driveway with his belongings. He said that Joy quickly accepted the change and after all three discussed whether he wanted to make his bedroom downstairs or in the living room, he chose the living room and they all began moving furniture.

He said the atmosphere was fine for the first couple of days. Joy worked all the time, but on rare occasions, they were able to talk. After they talked about Zaden's Mom having had several children by different fathers, Joy made a smart remark, probably trying to be funny, which did not settle well with Zaden. He said at first the arguments were small and unemotional, but over time, they became more frequent and more intense, over what he thought were trivial things. He said Joy was very paranoid about Zaden's motorcycle and his long hair and "gang' appearance and she was concerned that he would attract attention from the wrong people—people from Geoff's past. He said he tried to appease her and got his haircut short, military-style, parked his bike around the side of the house out of plain view, and stopped wearing his black and white gang color dew rags. He said he never wanted to be a gangster but explained that Geoff had told him a lot about many gangs, and the stories fascinated him.

He explained to the court how much he contributed to the household immediately after his arrival. He said he never just handed over the money, but he would fill the gas tanks of both vehicles, buy the dog food, even paid to treat all five dogs of whooping cough, and paid for other miscellaneous things like that. He said his original intention was to help his dad around the house, and that getting a job was way down on the list of things to do. He was getting a military check that covered his bills, but as soon as he arrived, he realized Geoff and Joy were having financial difficulties, so he went to work rather quickly after his arrival. He said that he had given Geoff a couple of hundred dollars to go toward his truck payment once, but found out later that Joy never got any of that money, and the truck payment did not get paid.

He said as a city boy; it was hard for him to drive in the mountains. He said he got confused easily and would sometimes take rides on his motorcycle, so he could try to figure out the main routes. He confirmed that Geoff was exchanging his painkillers with Pam for weed, and that he had gone twice to her house for the exchange, but that Geoff would not take him to other drug exchanges. He told some interesting stories about Geoff; giving him credit for up to twenty-two murders over his lifetime and that Geoff was the best meth cook across the country. Zaden told that his dad had a one-million-dollar bounty out on him after he turned all those people in, and he was published in a book about biker gangs since Geoff got off the charges of cooking meth. It was then that the locals figured out that it was Geoff who squealed to the Feds. When Geoff had tried to buy the gun, and the federal agents talked to him, and eventually took him out of the program, the agents were convinced that no one was even looking for him, much less being a threat to him. After all, it had been twenty years or so since all that stuff had happened.

When the questions came around about the day that Joy was shot, Zaden seemed to have a bad memory. He explained that he had just received his first paycheck the weekend that Geoff killed Joy on September 6th. His shift that morning started early as he was still in training, but he remembered getting home around 2 or 3 in the afternoon. The police had his work records on file that coordinated when he punched in and out, which backed up his story so far. He mentioned that he had decided he was going to move back home, and he planned to save all the money he made to get a U-Haul and drive back west. He had called his Mom to ask her for the money, but she could not afford the rental of nearly $2,000. She told him she would work toward getting it for him, but that he needed to save for it too.

He said that when he arrived home that day, he saw Geoff working on one of the trucks and he walked over to talk to him. He said he does not remember Geoff's behavior, but that Geoff soon told him that he had murdered his wife. Zaden said he thought his dad was joking with him, but Geoff was talking nervously about moving to Canada and finishing fixing the trucks so that they could move. When asked if his dad was crying as he talked about killing his wife Zaden said he could not remember. (I personally think he would remember if his bad biker dad, who he idolized, was crying or not). He said he went inside, through the upstairs door, and changed his clothes. When he returned outside, Geoff was pretending as if he was sick, although he was not clammy and walked fine on his own.

They went into the house, upstairs, and Zaden helped his dad to the couch, near the air conditioner, fixed him a sandwich, and brought him a glass of water. Up to this point, Zaden had not gone downstairs and had not seen Joy. He said it was about 45 minutes before Geoff told him he wanted to show Zaden something. They both headed downstairs, Zaden was in front, and Geoff was behind him, and as soon as they turned the corner into what was called the man cave, Zaden saw Joy on the couch with multiple gunshot wounds all over her torso. He said she was leaning onto the arm of the couch, and she did not look normal; she was motionless, not breathing. He said he went over to feel for a pulse, and when there was none, he started to panic and wanted to leave the room. As he was trying to make his way to the back door, he said Geoff pulled a gun, pointed it right at him, and said, "You are going to help, or you are going to join her." He said from that moment forward, Geoff always referred to Joy as an "IT" and never again considered her a human being, but rather an object. Zaden said his dad made him help dispose of the evidence, and Zaden kept thinking that if he could kill his wife, he could or would certainly kill him if he did not do what he was told.

Zaden said he did everything his dad instructed him to do. He said he did not think about Joy's family or the law, but instead, was very convinced that his dad could shoot him at any time. His memory got shady around this time. He could not remember who got the tarps, duct tape, and ratchet straps. He said he reinjured his back when he tried to move her body from the couch to the floor, but he kept on working. He helped his dad move the furniture from the room to the fire pit, using a dolly, and once the room was cleared of all the furniture, wall pictures, curtains, etc.; they started rolling Joy's body with two or three tarps and taping them with duct tape. He said they started at the feet and rolled and wrapped and taped her from the feet, then the torso, and then the head. He could not remember how many or what color the tarps were. He could not recall if she was limp or stiff, or if she bled out or not, but once they were finished, they checked to make sure there were no gaps in the tarps to allow body fluids to escape. Zaden too, swore that he had no knowledge of any dismemberment, cutting, gutting or anything else like that. He did say that he was very surprised at the knowledge Geoff exhibited throughout the process as if he had done this before. Zaden said Geoff was talking all the time about having connections with the bikers and that he wanted to re-enter the gang.

The judge asked for a short break, and after we returned, Zaden kept saying he did not want to do this but that he was afraid of his dad. He said Joy was a nice person, and she did not deserve this, and as he was digging the grave, and his dad telling him to get into it to see if it was deep enough, he considered that psychological intimidation. He said his dad kept asking him to take the fall if the police caught them. He kept saying that if he (Geoff) went to jail, someone would kill him because of his past, and kept telling Zaden that the gun was his and it could be traced back to him, etc. After they got Joy into the truck, Geoff told Zaden to clean the room thoroughly with the industrial-strength bleach. He was told to clean everything—floors, walls, ceiling, everything. When asked to coordinate dates and times with the events he was remembering, Zaden could not do it. He said he called work to say he was not coming in and that his dad wanted him to quit his job. Geoff began talking that he did not want Zaden to move back home, and Zaden began to feel trapped.

It was about this time, when questions about the burial and the police visits and so forth where Zaden answered most of the questions with, "I cannot remember". He could not remember the route they took to the makeshift gravesite, or if Geoff kept in touch via the phone anytime they separated, or what tools they took to use to bury her. The only thing he did remember is that it was a full moon and if that information is the truth, Joy was buried the night that the deputy showed up to perform the welfare check, on September 9, 2014. Throughout his entire testimony, he spoke badly of his dad and was sure to put all the blame on him. He said each time an official would talk to him privately; he refused to tell on his dad because he was so scared that Geoff still had connections, and if Geoff went to jail, someone from the biker gang would kill him or his family members. He confirmed that he told his jail cellmates that he shot and killed Joy and that he and his dad were going to split the life insurance policy. He said he told the story so that the other inmates would not bother him. He could not remember how he knew the dollar amount of the life insurance policy. All three of the lawyers had their turn asking Zaden questions, and when he returned to his seat, his mother, Tonya, was called to the stand.

Tonya Testifies

Tonya said that she was Geoff's wife from 1988–1990. She had one daughter when they got married, and the two had Zaden, who she raised from birth to eighteen years old. At eighteen, Zaden moved in with her brother and stayed with them for a short while before going into the army. She confirmed that Zaden was fanatical at trying to find Geoff. He had always been fascinated by all the biker stories Geoff's brothers, and other bikers would tell, and he started trying to find Geoff when he was a young teenager. Tonya kept begging Zaden to stop looking for him and explained the abuse she received from him the entire time they were together. She told Zaden that Geoff beat his first son from another woman and that the man was no good. As a matter of fact, she said several times that Geoff was just pure evil.

During the questioning, Tonya explained that she had a brain injury that would prevent her from recalling things, but she would try her best to answer the questions asked. The lawyers wanted to know if Zaden had called her to borrow money to return home. She said, "*Yes, he did,*" but she and her current husband had just helped another child and could not afford to help him right away. She said she told Zaden that she would work hard to save the money, but could not foresee getting it before October or November, and told Zaden to start saving what he could too. She told how she begged and begged Zaden not to visit Geoff when he contacted the family in 2014, but Zaden wanted to meet his dad. She also begged him not to move in with Geoff, but Zaden did not listen. She confirmed that Zaden was about two years old when Geoff went into the Federal Witness Protection Program.

Tonya said that the next thing she knew, Zaden was calling her from jail, on October 23rd. When she met with the primary investigator, she told him how Geoff treated her when they were together years ago. She said Geoff was pure evil, manipulative and very violent. She said that Zaden became violent, depressed, and constantly had mental problems throughout all his school years because he felt abandoned by his father. She said Zaden made good grades and was smart, but had relationship problems with the people around him. Zaden had become violent with her as he got older, and even had an altercation with a sergeant when he was in the army. She said that Zaden built this fantasy that Geoff was a great person and wonderful dad, and he never believed any of the stories she told him about how his dad abused her. Tonya was confused easily by the questions being asked, and unable to keep track of dates or times, so after all the lawyers and prosecutors asked the few questions they had for her, she was dismissed.

Near the end of the day, the prosecutors rested, and Geoff and Zaden's lawyers moved to deny all the charges. There was some bickering back and forth between the prosecutors, the other lawyers, and the judge, but after all was discussed, the judge said that closing arguments would be the next day. He explained that we would begin again at 9 a.m., and he would give the jury their instructions at which time they could begin deliberating the facts presented to them at this trial.

One afternoon, near the end of the trial and during a lunch break, my son and I had packed our lunch. He was sitting inside the truck communicating with his girlfriend, so I went outside to give him some privacy, dropped my tailgate, and I was eating my lunch in the parking lot of the courthouse. I did not know that earlier that morning, I had parked my vehicle close to Tonya's car, and on this particular day, Tonya stopped a short distance away from my tailgate to catch my attention. She smiled and said, "Hi," and asked permission to step closer and talk with me. Of course, I gave her permission. I had no animosity toward her, as a matter of fact, I felt very sorry for her. The fact that her twenty-some-year-old son would not listen to his mother was not her fault, and my heart ached for what she was going through.

Tonya began telling me she was so very sorry for what had happened to Joy. She said she had gotten to know a little about her through her daughter who had visited Joy and Geoff and through some conversations she had with Zaden. Tonya said she was so sorry for our loss. I thanked her for her kind words, we hugged, and both of us cried a little. All I could say in return was that this thing should have never happened. I kept saying he should have listened to his mother and that this thing should have never happened. It was a sad situation all the way around, and the only two that did not seem very bothered by it were on trial.

Chapter Fourteen

October 22, 2015

None of the family slept well that night, and most of us had the jitters and anxiety, like when you are excited because something is about to happen but scared as to what the outcome was going to be. I started praying long and hard both that night and the next morning, and by the time my son and I were walking out of the door to return to the courthouse, I felt confident and assured. I was calm and had a peace above all understanding, and I could not help but smile. My son was jittery, as was my dad, brother, his girlfriend, and I kept trying to reassure them that things were going to turn out for the justice of Joy.

On Thursday, October 22, 2015, the jury received an explanation and given thirty different jury instructions. The judge was thorough and detailed, making sure that the foreperson and all others fully understood the charges against Geoff and Zaden, what each meant, and how they should view the charges with the evidence presented. There was one short break in-between the jury getting all the instruction, but by 2:23 in the afternoon, the judge chose from a hat, the names of the two alternates, and he thanked the alternates for their time and attention and released them from duty. The jury was then asked to return to the backroom for deliberation, and the judge made himself available, should they have any questions at all.

The verdict was received a few minutes after 4 p.m. Again, this was God's perfect timing; the verdict would happen on the same day and almost the same hour when Joy's body was found exactly one year earlier. The jury was given a list of ways that they could charge the two defendants should they find them guilty. It was rather complicated because Geoff and Zaden were charged together for the crimes, and had four pending charges against them. The charges were listed as first-degree murder, conspiracy to commit murder, murder with a gun, and concealing a dead body. The list of sentencing guidelines started with the toughest sentence first and worked down to the lesser sentences.

When they returned to the jury box, the foreperson was asked if everyone agreed to a guilty or not guilty charge, and if they had agreed to the sentence to be imposed, and she said, "Yes, unanimously." She then read that the jury found both defendants guilty of all four charges. Joy's family quietly shook each other's hands and high fived each other, while Tonya, Zaden's mom, let out a cry and started sobbing. I felt sorry for her because her young son was now found guilty of first-degree murder.

The judge then asked the foreperson if the jury had reached a sentencing decision. She again said they were unanimous in their selection and told the judge and the courtroom that their sentence recommendation was "Life without the possibility of parole, plus a $100,000 fine." In addition, the foreperson said the jury would like to recommend an additional ten years for conspiring to kill Joy, another five years for transporting her body and concealing it from family and police officials, and finally, an additional three years for the use of a firearm to commit murder. The judge considered the additional charges and added them to the record and final recommendation of the jury. Once again, Joy's family showed approval as Tonya sobbed.

As the judge explained, he would have to look over the case with a fine-toothed comb to make sure every inch of the trial was conducted within all the boundaries of the law. He explained that he was the one that actually had the final sentencing decision, and he was not legally allowed to increase the sentencing recommendation of the jury (which in this case could not have been increased anyway, since the jury gave them the strongest and most severe sentence available by law). He did, however, have the power to reduce the sentence as he sees fit. He set the final sentencing date for February 8, 2016.

The prosecutors told the judge that even at the end of the trial, neither of the defendants showed any remorse for what they had done. He reminded the judge that they butchered my sister and still showed no remorse. He added that Zaden was still misbehaving after having been incarcerated, listing several additional offenses such as finding a weapon, writing racial remarks on the prison property, and racially fighting. The defense attorneys argued that the judge should consider the minimal charges allowed by law. The guidelines set by law for Geoff ranged from forty-five to seventy-five years, while Zaden's indicated a lighter sentence of twenty-three to thirty-nine years. It may be that Geoff's sentence range was higher because of his past criminal history, but I do not understand many laws.

For instance, the transporting and concealing the body (regardless of how the criminals mutilate or handle the corpse) has a maximum sentence of three to five years. At the time of this writing, we are going on four years since the occurrence, and I am just now starting to have days where I am not emotionally distraught by this loss. Moreover, when I say loss, by far, it was the not knowing where her body was that was the hardest for me to cope with. Do not get me wrong, I thought it was unthinkable that someone would want to kill Joy, but as I have said before, this crime occurred for the love of money.

The judge then set a date for his final sentencing and thanked the jury for their lengthy time and astute attention. He explained the honor and privilege of sitting on a jury panel and thanked them, especially because this trial was particularly gory, and it lasted days longer than originally anticipated. As he dismissed them, and they all rose to exit the room, I began to clap, but the prosecutor, my family, and then the judge quickly and sternly reprimanded me for my actions. I had clapped because I wanted the panel of jurors to know, I too appreciated their attention, their time, and their decisions.

Chapter Fifteen

The Victim Impact Statements

Before the trial ever began, the family had gotten information about a part of the trial called the victim impact statement. They explained to all of us that we, being a victim of the crime by losing our family member, had the legal right to write how this crime affected our lives. We were told that the judge would read what we submitted, as well as both defendants, their lawyers, and of course, the prosecution team, but the jury could not hear our statements. The victim impact statements occurred after the guilty verdict was rendered. Dad and Mom paid for Joy's cremation and funeral, so they could also submit the financial burden this crime caused them. Mom, of course, could not verbalize how the crime affected her, but my dad tried to explain it to the best of his ability. I urged my son and brother to write something up, but both of them said that since Geoff and Zaden were going to get to read the impact statements, they did not want the two to get the satisfaction of learning how this crime affected them.

I, on the other hand, thought of this process a little differently. My victim impact statement was a shorter version of the writing here, particularly the important dates and highlighting some of the trauma I felt when I found the spine. I ended the writing with a short paragraph explaining to the judge what I hoped would be the outcome of this trial. The last paragraph read something like this:

> My hopes are that Geoff and Zaden get the maximum sentences as the consequence for the selfish and horrific crimes they committed. I pray they both ask Jesus for forgiveness and that they will participate and contribute to prison ministry (for the rest of their lives) as atonement for the sins they committed. I have faith in your wisdom and judgment, Your Honor, and trust God will guide you through your decision of sentencing them for the crimes of murdering and then concealing the body of my sister, Mom's daughter, and Tom's Aunt Joy.

I had written a poem to Geoff throughout the ordeal, but only after a Bible verse kept running through my head. The purpose of writing the poem was to let Geoff know that I knew what he had put my sister through during their marriage, and I felt a strong urge to wash my hands of them, so to speak. After talking things over with the Lord, I sat down and wrote the poem. The verse that kept running through my head was Ezekiel 3:18 (KJV), which reads like this:

> When I say unto the wicked, Thou shalt surely die; and thou givest him not warning, nor speakest to warn the wicked from his wicked way, to save his life; the same wicked man shall die in his iniquity; but his blood will I require at thine hand.

This was telling me that in order to "wash my hands" of them, I needed to let them know that God loved them, and they could, at any time, ask Jesus to forgive them and change their ways. This is the poem I was able to read to them during this impact statement phase of the trial:

> Geoff,
>
> I never liked you from the beginning
>
> But man, Joy loved you every day
>
> And I bet if she could, she told you that
>
> As she bled on the couch, where she laid
>
> She worked her sixty plus hours a week
>
> And through her money you blew
>
> All the while getting government funds
>
> Of which she never knew
>
> Since you wouldn't work, disability she tried
>
> She'd make the calls and argued your case
>
> She pleaded and begged you to help her
>
> She got tired of running the race
>
> You made her swallow her pride
>
> When to her family she went

And through her tears, she asked for help
To pay for the truck or the food or the rent
Joy tried so hard to please you
She worried about your health
She cried she didn't want to lose you
She gave 100% of herself
She got you into that medical trial
That helped your liver to cure
And you got healed, a long healthy life
to spend in prison for murdering her
Love for money is the root of this evil
Despite all the love that she gave
You took the life of my sister
And put her in a makeshift grave
And for taking her life, you expected pay?
Life insurance, beneficiary, your name
My sister was so much smarter than you
Almost always one step ahead of the game
You wouldn't even be the man to protect her
To stop the disrespect from your son
You allowed this thing to happen
Whether you did or did not shoot the gun
You took away the only one on this earth
That thought you were worth the time
And because you conspired to kill her
You stand here now to pay for your crime
Her blood her cries and the smell of her death
And Pork Chop's sad behavior too

Will haunt you every day and night

And they will go to the grave with you

Her family and friends sure do miss her

Her memories will keep all of us strong

Meanwhile, you will be tormented

Behind bars where you belong

Through God's grace to this end, we stand

And our prayers were all answered true

This Honorable Judge now holds your future

On this earth, you will pay your dues

And one day we WILL ALL meet our maker

I pray Joy's love will see her through

But you'd better consider God's judgment

And ask forgiveness for the sins that you do

God's forgiveness is yours for the asking

And passing judgment is not my place

We all have to pay for our choices and

Forgiveness is found in God's grace

You have free will to seek Jesus Christ

Joy is gone—we all have sorrow to pay

Know this fact: **we will all answer to God**

So, heed my warning about judgment day.

When I wrote the poem, I was hoping that what I wrote would come true about Geoff feeling torment and haunted by what they did, when in reality, I know that they are not bothered by any of it. In fact, even before the trial had begun, when Geoff was in the county jail that was right beside the place where I was teaching, he had struck up a relationship with one of the female inmates. Even though it was against the law to do so, he and she had started writing back and forth to each other and had started making plans for a future together.

The way I understand it, Geoff would send his letters to her mom's house, who would carry them to her daughter to read. First, why would a mother want her daughter talking with anyone in jail, much less one who was accused of first-degree murder of his wife? I can only imagine that both of them were suckered into Geoff, "just trying to help his son" routine that he kept trying to sell to everyone else. My thought about that includes, *why not take the whole rap then?* After all, Geoff is a sickly old man, who cannot live life without someone else taking care of him, and his son is young, not having the opportunity yet to live life. Why not take all of the blame and give his young son a chance to have a life, of course, that is how I think a really good Dad would do, like Jesus, and I am grateful that God's justice included Zaden going to prison too.

Chapter Sixteen

Final Sentencing Day

On February 8, 2016, Joy's family was once again in the courtroom, hopefully for the last time. The judge confirmed that all persons read the Victim Impact statements that Dad and I had submitted, and the prosecutor insisted that the judge add a $5,009 restitution charge to the defendants for reimbursing Dad and Mom for the cost of the cremation and funeral. The judge said he read Geoff's two-page letter about how cruel he thought solitary confinement was, and it was brought to the court's attention that Geoff had received a certificate in Bible lessons since the last time he was in the courtroom. The lawyer for Zaden tried to explain away the misconduct of Zaden, (the fighting, weapons found in his cell, racial problems, etc.), and said that all of his life he defended himself when he was bullied. I questioned to myself, "*Then, why did Zaden not defend himself from his puny and sickly dad when he held the gun to him?*" I never did buy that "being afraid of his dad" story.

Then, the judge took control. He said he reviewed the trial records and absolutely everything was conducted legally and justly, and the two had received a fair trial. He said there was sufficient evidence that in this crime we lost a human being, Joy, and the sad part was, we lost her by violence from the people she should have felt the most comfortable around, and in her own home where she should have felt the safest. He said the two should feel shameful by how they mutilated her corpse and for hiding her in the makeshift grave, causing her family overwhelming worry, sorrow, fear, and anxiety by not knowing where she was.

He said that after reviewing all evidence, he simply could not reduce the recommended sentences given by the jury for such a savage crime. In addition, he added an additional three years of post-supervision to each of the other charges, listed as ten years for conspiracy, five years for concealing the body, and three years for using a firearm to commit a felony, over and beyond their life in prison without parole sentence and the $100,000 fine. All the charges were to run consecutively. Both defendants told the court that they would appeal the decision. The lawyers that assisted the two throughout the trial, each removed themselves, and both defendants were told they would get two new lawyers to handle any appeals or future court proceedings.

In March of 2016, a television network got in touch with the prosecution team, asking if the prosecutor would talk to them about the case. They wrote me an e-mail. I talked it over with my brother Laith, my son Tom, and of course, Dad, to get everyone's opinion. We all unanimously agreed that we did not want Geoff and Zaden to get any kind of recognition for what they did. By this time, all of Joy's family and friends knew that Geoff was narcissistic and would have loved to have the case and his handy work shown on a television show. I wrote the prosecution team back and respectfully declined their sharing any of the case details with the network representative. We have not heard any more from them, although we are fully aware that the case is now part of the public record but would hope that networks would respect the family wishes as to not give either of the criminals' attention for the crimes they committed.

Chapter Seventeen

God Is Working

My sole purpose for writing this was two-fold. First, to get some of the thoughts out of my head and onto paper as a way to minimize the effects they have on my emotions and memory. Equally as important to me is noting how God was such a huge part of the justice in this case. It seems like He was working toward the justifying end even months before this event ever happened.

It was May of 2014 when I got the strong urge to move closer to my parents. That was the last thing I wanted to do. I was sickly to a point where I thought I was dying, and I certainly did not want to move and be a burden to my parents. My primary doctor, as well as the pulmonary specialist, was telling me my congestion and inability to breathe was from Chronic Obstructive Pulmonary Disease (COPD), and they kept recommending I go on pure oxygen, 24/7, but that was out of the question to me. However, at the same time, I could barely walk from my couch to the kitchen and had been unable to breathe regularly for months. The Lord weighed heavy on my heart giving me only thoughts of how I could have a yard sale and sell many of my possessions, and that Dad needed help taking care of Mom since Joy was unable to help. I prayed and even cried that I did not want to make the move, all the while, putting price tags on my possessions and preparing for a week-long yard sale. I moved in June, and within weeks of moving, my congestion and lung issues subsided. Come to find out, I had been breathing in mold, and that was what was causing my breathing issues. So, the move was a two-fold blessing, one to get me out of the mold, and two to get me near my parents and Joy. My sister was murdered in September, and I was the only one living nearby who was physically able to put up the fliers and do the things necessary (except for Geoff and Zaden—who of course, had no interest in looking for her).

One of the wonderful things about moving south was that my sister and I could get together occasionally when we could arrange the time. I was a full-time college student who at the age of sixty plus found it harder to learn than it had ever been before, so school took up much of my free time, reading and re-reading, writing and re-writing. I was also helping with Mom and Dad, having a standing date to do the house cleaning on Saturday mornings, while Dad went grocery shopping for the week. I also had about an hour's commute back and forth to my teaching job, so arranging free time with Joy's busy schedule was a difficult thing to do. She worked one full-time and one part-time job all the time, and occasionally picked up a smaller part-time job during the summer months.

Joy and I had different personalities. I grew into this logical person, who has both feet on the ground, paying my bills when I receive them, and I rarely dream or fantasize about things that I feel could not happen. My sister on the other hand, always from a child until her death, dreamed about winning the lottery, starting a new business, inventing a new product, and seemed to have her head in the clouds all the time. She was fabulous to be around when we were younger, back during the years when children are *required* to daydream and use their imagination and think about what they wanted to be when they grew up. I loved talking to her then, and she and I had some wild imaginations, always laughing, and carrying on! We went to college together and competed for the best grades, but of course, she always won hands down. She could simply read the textbook about a subject, comprehend, and retain it, while I had to have two or three textbooks on the subject and study hard to make sense of it. However, over the years, I taught myself to listen to her conversations partially because more times than not, they consisted of dreams or fantasies. Today, regardless of what I preconceive about people, I have chosen to try to listen intently to anyone that is talking to me, whether it is reality or daydreaming that they are discussing.

I remember one day when she had stopped by, I was standing at the kitchen sink, and Joy was telling me what her computer password was to enter into her computer. I had no intentions of going onto her computer, I could not figure out any reason for me to know such information, and could not for the life of me, remember what started that conversation. Because the password she told me happened to be the name of her son's favorite movie when he was growing up, I can only assume that we had originally started talking about him. So, as I often did, I was letting this conversation run into one ear and out the other because it seemed irrelevant to me, and coincidently, it took me a night worth of thinking to remember her password when several weeks later the investigators asked me if I knew the password to her computer and when they were trying to get access to it. Isn't the Lord wonderful in His mysterious ways?

My sister's son had not been around for many years, but Joy always remembered his birthday and would call and talk to me on or near that day every year. In 2014, his birthday fell just a week or so before her murder, and when she called and asked if I had found him on any social media sights, this time when I told her no, I actually lied to her. In fact, my son and I had been talking to him for several months. I told him about his Mom and the rest of our family and asked if I could tell Joy or other family members that we were communicating, but he had told me no, so I was respecting his wishes. I think that God somehow had a hand in the fact that her son was visiting in a nearby town, the week before Joy was murdered. She had spoken especially lovingly about him during the 2014 phone call as if the close proximity had warmed her heart even more than normal, even though she did not know he was near.

My son discovered that her son was visiting his father's family nearby when Tom went to her son's social page. When Tom told me that her son was in the local area just days after we found out she had been missing, it originally sparked a strong hope that perhaps they had found each other, and that Joy had left with him to return to his hometown. Unfortunately, when the investigators checked out the possibility, her son knew nothing about her being missing, and they concluded he had nothing to do with it. It was just a strange and unexplainable timing of his nearby visit the week before her demise... or was it God bringing the love of those two hearts together, one last time?

Another conversation between my sister and me, which proved valuable happened within two weeks before her death. I was asking her which way she drove from her home to her two jobs in the next town several miles away. She said she preferred to drive the back roads, whereas, I am a highway driver, and I suggested to her during that conversation, to calculate the driving distance and the times of the two different routes—the back roads verse the highway, to see if she could save herself some time. Because of this previous conversation, on the day we learned she had been missing, I found it necessary to print a road map of the back roads because my original thought was that she wrecked on one of those twisty and hilly roads.

I have mentioned once throughout this writing about the Thursday she called during her lunch to confirm we were going to split the case of chicken quarters and during that phone call, I mentioned she needed to get her mail at a time when she had enough energy and could get across that busy street. Saying that reminded her to change her beneficiary on her insurance policies, and as it turned out, she must have hung up the phone, gone straight to her desk, and took care of the beneficiary business, because Friday was the first full day, which made the change official, and Saturday was the day she was murdered. And when I sent her a text that Sunday, my heart pinged worry.

There are so many little things like these conversations and events, which make me know that God was working a plan. We know that God does not stop evil from happening, but we also know that He can take the evil and make something good come from it. We also know that God is love and that God loves truth and justice, so He was on the scene and working a plan in my life and Joy's life, way before this tragedy ever happened. Even during the ordeal, while things were happening, I was often on my knees begging Him to help us; but I can see in retrospect that **He** brought this whole ordeal to its end and the final justice for Joy.

The first and what I consider a major answer to prayer was manifested three days after I prayed for the correct words, I could speak during the TV interview. I was desperate to find her body, and my sincere prayer was heard by the Lord. I asked Him to please convict the heart of those who knew where she was to tell the police. Three days after I prayed it, Geoff was being questioned in the interrogation room, and after the investigators continued to ask him, he said they would need a shovel—he was taking them to her body. What about the cell phone pings on Geoff's cell phone? He was talking at each of the locations during the time he was throwing out the three pieces of evidence, on the day he said he threw them out of the moving vehicle. What perfect God timing was that? Then, the way the items landed seemed a little too odd for it not to have been God's handy work. For the cell phone to be thrown from a moving vehicle and the case end up leaning against a tree stump, like the lucky leaner in a game of horseshoes. The purse was found standing perfectly on its bottom as if it had been sat down on the table; not laying, leaning, thrown over in the grass, but just sitting there, on the side of the road to be found within hours of her missing person's report being filed into the system.

By the way, the Holy Spirit bugged me until I finally decided I would call the sheriff's department that night! I had thoughts that they were busy, and I would be a bother because I just wanted to know if Geoff lied to the deputy, but I was agitated until I picked up the phone and called. God wanted that missing person's report filed because he knew the purse was going to be found the next morning. What about Him leading Joy to finally go to the DMV to renew her license months after arriving in the new state and for the picture to turn out rather good? Usually, the driver's license cameras catch your hair sticking up, one eye closed, or a twisted, malformed smile, but hers was good, and only one month old when it was needed the most.

Moreover, God and His absolute perfect timing showed again at the end of the trial. The jury's verdict came back on the same day and very near the same hour of the day when the police discovered Joy's body, one year earlier. October 22, 2014, her body was located, and the verdict to the trial was given October 22, 2015, both very close to 4 p.m. In addition, the numerical date of Joy's funeral was 12–13–14, the last sequential date of the twenty-first century, (without any intention of having her funeral on that numerical date). Also, her funeral was the Saturday before many churches in celebration; light the Advent candle for joy. Even though I am fully aware that the verb joy is different from the noun Joy, I could not help but think that so many persons would speak her name (Joy) to God. How awesome are those coincidences? I cannot be convinced that these occurrences were anything other than God loving my sister, manipulating principalities and powers, working a plan, and wanting justice done on Joy's behalf. I think God loved her so much because she was joyful and made so many people laugh and feel good. Finally, He is continuing to bless me every day with other revelations as well!

Since the murder, the Lord has helped me over other hurdles. While I was looking for her body, fall foliage started to drop. I kept asking the investigator each time I spoke to him, to try to find out what color clothing Joy was wearing at the yard sale. I kept asking him to talk to the person at the yard sale with whom she discussed the motorcycle because it was becoming almost impossible to distinguish the possibility of clothing from the colorful leaves now falling to the ground. Not only was the forest floor much more slippery, but the colors were also distracting, and I was going left or right toward oranges, reds, or yellows, thinking it was clothing only to discover it was leaves. Besides how frustrating it was becoming, and how tired we were already for the weeks of looking, the anxiety took away my love of the fall season. Instead of looking at the beautiful colors, I saw distraction, hindrance, and became very overwhelmed.

All my life, I had considered fall and especially the fall foliage, my favorite time of the year. Every year I would make a point to drive along mountaintops so that I could appreciate the beauty of God's handiwork. There were many loveable spiritual moments over my years that were just between God and me, in total amazement and total awe of His magnificence. I felt Him loving me as I was loving Him and basking in the beauty of the fall colors. It always brought me close to God and inspired worship, love, and admiration for His mighty hand and beautiful creation. However, in the fall season of 2015, the changing of the leaves just began a deep depression for me. The trial was going on, anxiety began over-whelming me, and without an official diagnosis by a professional, I would venture to say, perhaps some PTSD was included in my emotional roller coaster ride, and I did not even want to look at God's beautiful fall foliage. It was hard to get through the season. Then, in the fall season of 2016, I was driving a tractor-trailer truck when the season began, and as soon as I saw the leaves changing colors, the anxiety started to build all over again. I was doing a lot of thinking, crying, reliving our searching for my sister, and the changing colors of the leaves just made it worsen with each passing day.

One time, I started crying so hard that it was necessary to pull the truck over onto the shoulder of the road. I set my brakes, turned off the truck and I hung my head and sobbed for fifteen minutes or so, thinking about how difficult it was to distinguish leaf colors from possible clothing. Then, in a moment of clarity, I gathered myself, and I prayed to God with a most sincere heart. I said, "**Lord; please do not let these criminals take away a time and a season that You and I have shared for so many years. You know how much I have always adored Your masterpieces in the fall foliage and how much the beauty moves my heart and grows my love and admiration for You. I loved those times with You throughout my life, and I don't want these criminals to take that away from us. Please, Lord.**" Instantly, I felt love, comfort, and peace, and I heard a small voice call my name and say, "**I am going to show you some wonderful sights this year.**" It made me smile ear to ear, I gathered myself, and started praising God. I breathed deeply for a few minutes and went back to work. I was on my way home and finished out my day.

The next morning, I was dispatched to Maine and had pretty much forgotten my encounter and promise from the Lord. I am so embarrassed to say that I often forget the Lord's encounter, His words of encouragement or even special moments spent with Him. The ONE TRUE GOD spends time with me, shares moments, or teaching lessons, and I forget them? However, I do, and I did. I did not have that praying moment in my mind at all. Now my day did consist of praising the Lord and having worship music in the CD player and singing along, and I was loving God like I do most of my days, but that particular prayer and answer moment was not in my mind until I turned a corner and saw a mountainside that took my breath away. I literally felt my heart leap, a tear came to my eye, and I was awestruck.

The reds were more vivid than I had ever seen before; the contrasting colors of oranges, yellows, and pine greens looked like beautiful tapestry spanning the width of a mountain, and I was grateful that there was room on the side of the road to pull the truck over. I got my camera and snapped at least a dozen pictures, but as I looked at each one of them, I deleted them because none of them showed the beauty that I was seeing with my own eyes. None of the pictures did any justice to the beauty God was sharing with me at that moment. I took my lunch break there, enjoying the scenery and praising the Lord for His goodness. I knew from that moment on, I would no longer mourn, feel anxious, or get depressed with the fall season, and it was once again a special time between my God and me. I did see some beautiful fall foliage the whole rest of that season and the year of 2017 as well. Our God is a wonderful God, and He loves us.

There are other moments where the Lord has helped me through the grieving process of my sister. It was also in 2016 when I was quite depressed and doing a lot of crying and not much of anything else. I understood that some of my crying was selfish, simply because I missed her, but this time, I felt so terribly alone. More alone than I had ever felt at any time in my life. Joy was my fourth sibling, and my only sister to pass away. Therefore, I started praying about the loneliness. Up to this time in my life, I had not gone to too many churches, only on the rare occasions when I was visiting my aunts on a Sunday, did I ever go. I usually worked on the weekends; I never understood why it was necessary and was never drawn nor had any inkling to go to church. I read my Bible, I was spiritual, spirit-filled, loved God, gave Him the glory, praised Him, walked and talked with Him, and up to this point had no need for a church.

The more I prayed about the loneliness I was feeling, the more I asked God to help me understand it. I kept thinking it was because Joy was my only sister, or because she was my fourth sibling, and could not understand why I had never felt this alone before. One night, after my prayers and before I fell to sleep, the Lord told me very gently, "Now is the time to go to church." I remember sitting straight up in bed and speaking just above a whisper, saying, "Lord, you know I am shy. I am backward, awkward, and do not socialize well." After a few moments of silence, I said, "Are you sure?" He replied, "You will find fellowship there." A day or so later, I was talking to my doctor about perhaps going to a church, and she recommended a church a couple of miles from my house because she knew the preacher, and I started going to church.

The first church was full of nice people. They had things to do throughout the week, and I found myself staying busy helping with the weekly pamphlets, the upcoming arts and craft yard sale, and various other activities. I went to church every Sunday, and tried very hard to fit in, although I was (and still am) very naive about church routine or church etiquette. After a month or so, I noticed I was making a spectacle of myself. The preacher would ask one Sunday for prayer for so and so who had to go to the emergency room, and they did not know what was wrong with her. I would add her to my prayers and then the next Sunday the preacher would give praises that she was home with no complications and I would say aloud and worshipping—praise God, thank you Jesus, or Hallelujah, while everyone else sat quiet, looking at me. It did not take long at all to realize I might be in the wrong church because I like to thank God for answering prayers and helping people with health problems. He is an awesome God and deserving of our praise!

The second church I attended was perfectly fine with me praising the Lord, and actually, I had to get a little used to their enthusiasm. While I had read and truly believed in prophesying, and speaking in tongues, this was the first church where I ever experienced such things. I sincerely felt like this church, or at least the presence of the Lord, brought me closer to God. There were no activities throughout the week that kept me busy like at the other church, but there were nice people, and I offered my help wherever I saw a need.

In 2016, during a serious grieving time the Lord spoke to me, rather sternly, and told me to stop crying for the dead. He said to start praising and glorifying Him, first because He and I were alive, and then because His salvation plan ultimately promised that I would see my loved ones again. How wonderful a directive from GOD, this was! It sounded utterly simple, and I am here to tell anyone that you cannot

praise God and give Him sincere thanksgiving, and be depressed at the
same time! It is simply impossible. As soon as you start praising Him,
He lifts your heart and sends you joy, and almost immediately, your
mood changes. Praise God! He is an amazing God and loves us!

However, as this human does, over time, I forgot that directive
from the Lord, and I found myself sulking and crying again. It had been
a rainy day, and I had to get in the rain to go to an appointment with
my spiritual counselor, who had given me a homework assignment
to journal to God. In his instructions, I was to imagine myself at a
favorite place and to envision God joining me there. Upon God's
arrival, I was to journal a conversation with Him. Well, at home, I
sat down with paper and pen, and I chose a favorite overlook where
I frequented often. However, during my search for Joy, I had gone to
that overlook to see if she was rolled over the cliffs, and on that day at
the overlook, I ended up shouting her name and crying hard for her
there. I would shout her name and listen intently for a whimper or a
rustle of the leaves, hoping she was hearing me call her. It was there,
that day when I realized I was going to have to learn the timeframe
and stages of human decomposition.

To take that beautiful overlook, and then remember that sad
moment, it was a natural progression to start crying for her, sitting
there in my living room, trying to journal to God. All of a sudden,
a rather stern voice said to me, "Go to church. I have a message for
you." I knew it was the Lord, and I knew He was serious about me
going to Wednesday service, which when I checked the clock, was
going to start within just a few minutes. I looked over my clothes,
I knew I had hat-hair, but I had just enough time to brush my teeth
and run. On my drive to church, I apologized to the Lord for my
appearance, but I still had my sad countenance and was wondering
what God's message was going to be.

Lo and behold, the preacher began his sermon with three bullet
points.
1) Evaluate the present situation.
2) Give God the glory.
3) Start looking toward our future in heaven.

His sermon was specifically about people that complained all the time, and his remedy to the complainers was those previously mentioned bullet points. He said complainers needed to evaluate the current situation differently, change the complaint into praising the Lord for all He has done for us, and to stop thinking about all the things to complain about, and start thinking about our future in heaven. As plain as the nose on my face, it dawned on me, that God had told me this already.

1) Stop crying for the dead, (re-evaluate that my crying for Joy will not change things).
2) Give God the praise for being alive.
3) Think about our future in heaven (that we will see our loved ones again).

This time that message has stuck. I must admit that sometimes it is hard to start praising when I am feeling so blue, but if I just keep up the effort, God gives me peace, joy, comfort, and my mood absolutely changes to gladness and joy. Praise the Lord!

God has helped me with my loneliness, my grief, and I think I improved my social skills some while I was going to church, and I am content to do my worshipping and praising at home, or wherever life leads me. It may be that I will be led to church again, but for the time being, I do not feel any negative convictions or issues about not going. I trust God to lead me, and I know God is with me, even though I am not going to church.

At the beginning of 2017, I quit my job as a truck driver because the grief was consuming my life and because finding a place to pull over a tractor-trailer is not an easy thing to do and driving while crying is not a safe thing to do. I first received counseling from the local hospice organization, and the counselor there suggested I go to a health doctor to get a checkup.

It was January 2017 when my doctor told me I should try to get Social Security Disability (SSD) due to the health problems that were diagnosed. I knew that over the last few years, it had become impossible to do anything strenuous, walk any distance, or climb stairs. I knew I was having a difficult time breathing doing the simplest of tasks, but I kept saying it was because I was getting older. Since I had one year's worth of bills saved in my bank account, I decided to apply for the disability. After numerous rejections from the SSD administration, I took myself off my medications and began trusting God to a point where and now I am working part-time.

I carry around the poem I had written to Geoff, and any time I meet someone who tells about how another person has done them wrong, I testify to how sincerely important it is to forgive people. There are many verses, some straight from God's mouth, which instructs us to forgive others if we want His forgiveness. When the opportunity arises, I give a short synapse of how my sister was murdered, and I read them the poem I wrote. I let them know that they will live a better life if they can find it in their heart to forgive the person, and God would help them.

Forgiving does not mean condoning, and it does not mean that you have to become friends or even associate with the person that wronged you. Forgiveness cleanses your heart of hatred; it tells God that you understand that there are evil people in the world, and there are people who sin. Forgiveness humbles your heart and tells God that we will let Him see the truth and wisdom in the circumstance, and let God tend to it. Maybe, a person will find it helpful to do what I do when I think about the criminals that took my sister; I say a quick prayer that "God I give them to You," and I sing praises for God's love of the truth and justice. He will make things right. We will ALL stand in front of God to give an account, so it is best to forgive others.

I also tell people, when they are griping about their husband, wife, children, or someone in their life that they should remember they love them, and not to sweat the small stuff. Show them that you love them and tell them that you love them because death can happen to anyone at any time. I know that sounds morbid, but it is so very true. Without warning, the person you are complaining about can be taken away by a stray bullet, a swerving car, a fall down the steps, a heart attack, or any number of life-taking occurrences. Then it is too late to let them know how much you love and care for them. Regrets are a heavy load to carry.

I begin each day, and I use any blank moment in my brain, to praise the Lord. I am one of these people that whistle while I work, hum, or sing to the Lord, all the time. I give Him thanks and show Him appreciation first for loving us first and then for His salvation plan. I thank Him that He called me into His fold, and I take a moment to notice the clouds, look at a flower, or watch a mother and child interact with each other, and I show awe and wonder for the magnificent world, His wonderful plan, and His Holy Bible, which explains it all.

We all have choices. Where we put our energy is where we will get our results... And I choose to praise and thank my Lord for being Love. He created the world and all its beauty for us to enjoy, and He created us for Him to enjoy. He loves us. He loves truth and justice. He loves worship and praise. He listens to our prayers, and He is with us always. Give God the glory and praise. He is a wonderful God.

Amen!

If you do not have a personal relationship with God, He Loves you and is waiting for you. He sent His Son, Jesus Christ, to live and die for the whole world's sin, including yours and mine. Jesus was raised from the dead and is with God in heaven, making it possible for you to have a personal relationship with God. Believe the Bible and the gospel stories. Believe Jesus is God's Son; that He lived, died, and has risen. Then when you sincerely want Jesus to be your Lord and Savior, tell Him that you are a sinner, but you know He died for your sin also. Tell Him you want Him to be your Lord and Savior. He will send the Holy Spirit to live within you, and to help you in your walk through your life, in similar ways as He helped my family and me through this ordeal. He loves you. He is waiting for you. You should get to know Him. He is a wonderful God!

Amen!

References

The Holy Bible: King James Version [KJV]. 1999. New York: American Bible Society. Public Domain. https://www.biblegateway.com/versions/King-James-Version-KJV-Bible/#booklist

CPSIA information can be obtained
at www.ICGtesting.com
Printed in the USA
LVHW081807081119
636788LV00009B/833/P